IT'S MY DUTY, ISN'T IT?

IT'S MY DUTY, ISN'T IT?

The Plight of Carers
in Our Society

JILL PITKEATHLEY

SOUVENIR PRESS

ISBN 0 285 62884 4 hardback
ISBN 0 285 62885 2 paperback

Photoset and printed in Great Britain by
Redwood Burn Limited,
Trowbridge, Wiltshire

ACKNOWLEDGEMENTS

I am grateful to my family, to my friends and to my colleagues at Carers National Association for the support they gave me while I was writing this book. I want to thank most particularly the hundreds of carers whose experiences and thoughts I have quoted.

I should also like to thank the following for permission to quote from published material:

The Controller of Her Majesty's Stationery Office for *Community Care — An Agenda for Action* by Sir Roy Griffiths, for *Better Services for the Mentally Ill* (Government White Paper 1971), for *Growing Older* (Government White Paper 1981), for *A Positive Choice* by G. Wagner, and for an extract from the debate on carers in the House of Commons, 1st May 1986 (Hansard); Routledge & Kegan Paul for *A History of the Mental Health Services* by Kathleen Jones; and the King's Fund for *When I Went Home* by Jill Pitkeathley and Pat Gay.

CONTENTS

1 Identifying Carers and their Role

We might be forgiven for thinking that caring had just been invented, that it sprang into being, fully fledged, round about 1980. For only then did the word come into normal use, only then did it start to appear in the social work and medical press, and only then did some people (and it is still only some people) begin to be aware of carers and the important part they play in society.

WHAT IS A CARER?

In the context of this book, I feel that the most appropriate definition is 'someone whose life is in some way restricted by the need to be responsible for the care of someone who is mentally ill, mentally handicapped, physically disabled or whose health is impaired by sickness or old age'. The majority of those carers, though by no means all of them, will be living with the person for whom they are responsible. You can also be a carer if you are living nearby and visiting every day, if you are living some way away and visiting every weekend and, similarly, you may be a carer for limited periods of time only — say, when your mother comes to visit twice a year. For many people, the caring aspects of their lives do not stop when the person cared for goes into some kind of residential accommodation or into hospital.

Defining what it means to be a carer is fraught with difficulty, and for many people the definition above might

seem unacceptable. Perhaps you are only a carer if you feel
you are, your life is only restricted if you feel it is, and so on;
but it is the 'restriction on life' which is most important. For
the purposes of this book I shall talk about carers in that
sense, and since I hope that this book will be read by many
carers, I must also hope that they will find the definition
appropriate.

It is very important to point out that the word 'carer' is
often used quite loosely with reference to other kinds of
people — for example, social workers and staff in residential homes. This kind of caring, however, is of a very
different order from the sort of caring which is the subject of
this book. Similarly, there are kinds of caring which most
people do at some time in their lives, which are also of a
very different nature: for example, the care given by a
mother or father to a child during its growing-up years, the
care we may show to a sick neighbour, or the help we give
to a workmate at a time of personal crisis.

The essential differences between these kinds of 'normal'
caring and the kind I am writing about are these: firstly,
normal caring is time-limited in some way — either because
the child grows up or the sickness comes to an end, and,
secondly, there is some expectation of reciprocity — we
would expect that the neighbour would do the same for us
if we became ill or in need. For carers, neither 1of these
statements is relevant. There is no telling how long the
caring will last and it is almost exclusively 'one-way'.

Who are the Carers?

They come in all shapes and sizes and from all back-
grounds. No one really knows how many carers there are in
the United Kingdom today, but a study by the Equal Opportunities Commission in 1980 indicated that there were at
least one and a quarter million of them. Later research,
produced in the Greater Manchester Borough of Tameside,
set the number much higher, perhaps as many as three
million.

In 1985 a question was added to the General Household survey, designed to gather information about carers. The results, published in 1988, surprised everyone. One adult in every seven is providing informal care and one in five households contains a carer. The survey showed that there are about six million carers overall in Great Britain, with about 1.7 million caring for someone in the same household. Three and a half million of these carers are women and two and a half million are men, although women are more likely to carry the main responsibility of caring.

Carers look after handicapped children, young adults, handicapped adults and elderly people who may have physical disabilities or mental handicaps, or who may be disabled through a psychiatric disorder or chronic disease or suffering from a terminal illness. About two thirds of carers are looking after someone elderly and 42 per cent are themselves over retiring age.

How do you Become a Carer?

There was no choice.
Who else was there?
It's my duty, isn't it?
I couldn't let him go into one of those homes.
You can't turn your back on your mother when she needs you.

These are some of the things people say when asked how they became carers. In general there are two processes by which they take on the role: either it creeps up on them by degrees and they do not notice what is happening, or it comes upon them out of the blue, as the result of a sudden illness or accident.

Here are two examples of how caring begins. In the first, it was a gradual process, whereas in the second it happened almost overnight. In each case the main carer is a daughter-in-law.

My father-in-law died in 1980 and his wife developed amnesia after his death. Both my husband and I were employed at that time and had two teenage boys. By 1981 my mother-in-law was unable to shop alone, so every Friday night my husband took her to buy the necessities, so giving her an outing, too. He then cooked her an evening meal. On Mondays I would call and take her an evening meal and on Wednesdays I would go again. Sometimes in summer my husband would come too and cut her grass for her. This was the pattern for three years until she deteriorated further. We arranged for Meals on Wheels to call and I now started going there before work also as she couldn't be relied on to dress herself.

By 1984 we were desperate as she was not safe in her own home. Her neighbours would phone us in the middle of the night to say her lights and radio were on, and we would have to rush over there (we lived eight miles away). Clearly, it was time she came to us, and she moved in during 1984.

It has all been a nightmare. I had a demanding job and two teenage children to consider. At the same time my own mother was in a wheelchair awaiting a hip replacement. She came every Sunday and had to be transported each way. I managed to cope with mother-in-law and my job for two years, but now my life is all caring as I've had to give the job up and both my boys are away from home. I expect they are relieved because Grandma is now doubly incontinent and has just been diagnosed with stomach cancer. It is hell, there is no other word. I feel I am in the middle of a nightmare and have no escape until Grandma dies. We should have said years ago we couldn't manage, but it only started with Friday night shopping and that seemed so little to do for her.

The second carer had a different experience:

Up to a year ago I was working part-time to help pay our rates, as we were buying our council house and had raised two children and seen them through university. My father-in-law was then 88 years old and he was suddenly admitted to hospital with a gastric ulcer. While he was there they found out that, unknown to us, he had been in the habit of taking a lot of patent medicines, such as strong cough linctus, and the doctors thought he should no longer live alone. I gave up my job at a minute's notice and rushed round

*preparing a bedroom for him. My life changed more or less over-
night, but I accepted that he had to come to live with us, not
because I am particularly fond of him, but my husband, as the only
son, stands to inherit Dad's house so I couldn't very well be
awkward about it.*

*Little did I know how dearly I would pay for this rush to care in
nervous tension and suppressed rage that I can no longer do as I
please in my own house. I will not dwell on the physical problems
— the incontinence, the coughing and spitting into the kitchen
sink which goes on all day, the refusal to wash — I put all this
down to old age, and fortunately I have never been squeamish. The
worst thing is the way he rules my life. He lives his life by a strict
routine which I have come to know very well, and if it varies by
even five minutes I am shouted at. Meals are served on the dot,
bath night is every Saturday at exactly 9 p.m., bedtime is exactly
10 p.m., and so on. It is easier to comply than waste breath
arguing and have him shout, stamp his foot and bang on the table.*

*We fully expect this state of affairs to continue for another seven
or eight years, as longevity runs in the family. So far I have not
asked for tranquillisers or taken to drink and have kept my sense of
humour, but I may not be able to laugh at all in a few years' time.
God help all carers!*

It is important to note that in each of the cases above there
was very little question of the carers recognising themselves as carers before they took up the role. Where it
happens gradually, it comes up on the carer subtly, with
only small increases in the amount of care required. There
is no necessity to make plans and alternative arrangements
because each little addition to the burden is only a slight
advance, and the total number of individual tasks which
make up the package of commitment multiplies only
slowly, until the carer is so far into the caring situation that
she can no longer back out. From a period of minimal
commitment, through a stage of undertaking a gradually
increasing number of tasks, she has progressed unawares
to the point where 'full' caring is necessary.

In the case of the caring role being assumed suddenly, by

definition the carer has no time to plan for it, no time to think of the effect it will have on her life, and certainly no time to consider any alternatives.

What will also be apparent from the two cases is that there is almost invariably someone who is assumed by everyone concerned to be the person who will become the carer. Somehow or other, people in the family know that 'Jane' or whoever, will be the carer. This has probably never been mentioned, indeed it is highly unlikely that it has ever been discussed, but even so everyone knows it. It is often difficult to find an explanation for this, although sometimes it is obvious — possibly Jane lives nearest or has always been closer to mother or does not have a job.

In both of the cases above it was assumed that the female would become the carer and give up her job, even though she was not the blood relative. This, too, is fairly typical. Women make up by far the majority of carers and research has repeatedly shown that they receive less support from the services than do men who are involved in the provision of the same level of care. There does seem to be an expectation in society that it is appropriate for women to take on a heavier burden of care, particularly where caring for an elderly person or for a handicapped child is concerned. When men and women are compared as carers, men are almost always receiving more help, both from their own social networks and from services, whereas women are likely to be undertaking caring tasks without support.

Willingness to take on caring duties is, however, usually expected of a spouse, whatever his or her sex, especially if that spouse is either already retired or near retirement.

In the main, then, it is women who are expected to do the caring, although throughout this book there will be examples of male carers who also carry heavy burdens.

There have been changes over the years in society's thinking about who is expected to care. For example, in the 1950s and 1960s, it was the single daughter, with a job but no family, who was expected to give up her work to care for her parents as they became elderly. Two changes have happened in more recent years. First, there are far fewer single women than there once were and, second, there is more understanding of the fact that a woman may value her career as much as a man does. Consequently, the person who is expected to give up a job now will not be the single woman with a career but more often the married one who may be working part-time, as we saw in the two examples.

Why do People Become Carers?

Caring always takes place within the context of a relationship, which may be a close one like that of spouse, less close like daughter-in-law and father-in-law, or a more remote one as in the following example.

I have my great-aunt living with me. She is getting very difficult and my patience is wearing thin. She is really no relation to me, I suppose, as she was the sister-in-law of my grandmother.

Some carers are caring for more than one person, very often two or even three elderly parents, but also perhaps a spouse and a child.

I have two people in my care, my husband, who is 66 and suffering from senile dementia, and our daughter who is 37 and was born brain damaged.

Sometimes, too, carers may find themselves caring for someone who is no relative at all.

I am a widow, and had just retired in September 1985 when my neighbour of 72 died, leaving her husband aged 79 to cope with life after bereavement. I felt his memory wasn't as good as it could have been, but soon discovered it was really the onset of dementia and that his wife had been covering up for him. He had a daughter, but she had a good job in the south and had to return to it soon after the funeral. I started to keep an eye on Gordon, but I soon found myself going in there ten times a day, as it was impossible to trust him to do anything for himself and I was so worried about him leaving the

gas on. Some days I would return home thinking I couldn't go on,
and I rang his daughter several times, but it was clear she was not
going to do anything. I couldn't sleep and the worry and the
responsibility took their toll. But still I did it for two years until he
died. I couldn't opt out somehow.

This neighbour wanted to care, or felt obliged to do so,
and she was also available — which the daughter was not.
Being available at the time when caring is needed is one of
the common reasons for becoming a carer.

When you ask someone why they became a carer you are
likely to receive a reply like 'I love her' or 'It's my duty', and
the caring role does indeed seem to be taken on for reasons
which are a complex mixture of love and duty. This is why it
is 'the person closest' who is generally expected to take on
the task. In terms of a loving relationship this is perhaps
easy to understand. The son in the case study following did
not think twice about it, in spite of the distress it caused
him.

I am a 54-year-old male. Early in 1978 my wife and I went
through a very acrimonious divorce after 25 years of marriage. At
the same time my mother was informed that after waiting for seven
years the hospital was ready to replace both her knees. Obviously
someone had to care for her as she had been a widow for 40 years.
One of my sisters lives in Australia and the other had young
children, so that left me. Fortunately I loved my mother very
dearly and held her in great respect. I went to live with her. The
operations were successful in removing the pain of the arthritis but
reduced her mobility, and recovery was very slow. Being immo-
bile, her weight increased and urinary incontinence began. Old
people like flannelette sheets but urine does not, and no matter how
hard you try, the smell soon invades the house. Every month I
went to the surgery and got her tablets. I also asked for help, but no
joy!

In 1980 Mum had a stroke, spent three days in hospital and lost
the sight of one eye. Still no one came to see her. In 1981, after a
good row, I was given a supply of pads and incontinence pants.

They helped. In 1983 she began failing. Her doctor said he could not help but I asked for a second opinion. A senior geriatrician came and changed her sleeping tablets. She was 100 per cent better. He also recommended her for a place in a day centre twice a week — in essence an excellent idea, but in practice disaster. One morning the ambulance would call at 8.30 a.m., the next at 10.30 or later. I had to assume the earlier time and was constantly hurrying her through the long process of getting clean and dressed. After four weeks we had to give it up.

Soon her incontinence became continuous and she was quite senile. At long last I informed the doctor I couldn't cope. I suggested a catheter but was told they did not like to fit them because of infection. I insisted and they fitted one. What a relief! To say that the high point of my day was to see a litre of urine in the bag after a night's sleep sounds silly, but it's true. Also, after five years on my own I now had a daily visit from the district nurse. It was only ten minutes, but the joy of not feeling helpless was wonderful. Mum finally died peacefully later that year. I still haven't got over it but I can't regret my decision to care for her. I did it for love.

It is perhaps more difficult to understand how a feeling of duty to take on a caring role can persist, even where love is absent. Nevertheless, the moral imperative to look after a dependent person within one's family is alive and well in the United Kingdom in the 1980s, as the following examples will show — the absence of love does not apparently mean the absence of a sense of duty.

If my mother is sick I'll look after her, but don't ask me to love her.

I've never loved my mother really, and I think she has never cared about me — well, I suppose that's why I feel as I do about her. She has always been a cold woman. But when she had her stroke it honestly never occurred to me not to look after her. I'm 57 and had a good job as a nurse in the Middle East, but I gave it up when they sent for me. I will look after her till she dies.

I can't say it was a good marriage: he drank a bit and when we were younger we rowed a lot. He never respected me somehow. He was as nice as pie to his friends and workmates but a bit of a bastard at home, if you know what I mean. The kids wonder why I do it, but you can't not, can you? I married him for better or for worse.

In my work as Director of an organisation which supports and counsels carers, I come across this strong sense of duty very frequently. Often it seems to be compounded of the fantasies people have about what caring is going to be like. Somehow or other, carers feel that the caring process itself may heal a broken relationship or resolve a long-standing quarrel; they feel, often for no logical reason, that the marriage which has always been rocky will somehow be strengthened by the enforced time they have to spend together, that somehow the father they have always hated will become a sweet, grateful old man in the process of being cared for, or that the guilt they always felt because they had left their mother alone when she was widowed will be wiped out by becoming her carer. They appear to have an idealised picture of what life will be like and cannot be dissuaded from it. Of course, no one tries very much to dissuade them.

It sounds so silly when I think about it now, but I used to have this image of us sitting together in the afternoons. She would have her hair nicely done and I might be doing a bit of sewing. There would be a nice smell of baking and we'd be chatting about old times or about the grandchildren. I realise now that that is how I wanted things to be when I was a small girl and came home from school. I wanted mother to be sitting waiting for me with cakes in the oven and ready to listen to my tales of school. Only she never was there, she was out working, and when she did come home she did nothing but shout anyway. Maybe I thought that we could make up for all those afternoons. Well, it was a rude awakening. You can't chat with someone who is senile, and when she wets herself I shout at her as much as she once shouted at me.

But there is another important factor in the willingness of people to take on the caring role, and that is the absence of any acceptable alternative. Most spouses feel that they must take care of their dependant, but many sons and daughters may feel that the ideal arrangement might be a good residential home where the parent could be looked after well and receive frequent visits from the family. This, too, may prove to be a fantasy — either simply not available or available only to those with large amounts of money.

We were living here in Essex, but my Mum was still up in Doncaster. We started to get calls from her neighbours about her wandering at night. When we came up to sort things out, I went to have a look at some of the homes around there. She said she'd really rather go somewhere like that than stay on her own, and quite honestly I just never thought of her coming to us at that stage. When I went to look at the places, it was another story. I just couldn't let her go in any one of them. They were full of really ga-ga old folks, shouting out and wetting themselves, and she couldn't even have a room to herself. So then we thought of moving her down here and I looked about here. But the prices! The only home I thought was suitable was going to cost £500 a week, so it was out of the question. That's how she ended up with us. We had the spare room so there was no excuse really.

Because of the strong moral pressure which many of us feel about caring for our dependent relatives, assumptions are made about the onus of responsibility, not only by carers themselves but also by people around them — their friends, neighbours and, most of all perhaps, by the professionals with whom they may come into contact. In 1987, the National Council for Carers and their Elderly Dependants published a short report called 'Can a carer say no?' After a press release in local newspapers, more than 500 letters were received by the Council. Only ten per cent of the carers who wrote in felt they had been given any kind of choice at all. For most, the assumption was simply made and they took on the role without question. In Chapter 5 I shall look more closely at the assumptions which professionals make about carers.

What Relationships give rise to Caring?

It seems clear that a spouse is expected to feel a duty to become a carer. This is always true of a female spouse and nearly always true of a male, although not when he is fairly young and has a demanding job. Certainly, if the male spouse has retired, there appears to be no question but that he should do the caring. Indeed, age or illness appears to offer no excuse for getting out of the caring role, with the result that a great many frail and elderly people are themselves acting as carers for spouses who are even more frail or elderly. It is not unusual to encounter carers who are in their eighties or even nineties.

If no spouse is available, then the duty apparently falls on a daughter or daughter-in-law. Although not blood relations, daughters-in-law seem to be expected to take on the caring role if no daughter is available. The son is seen as having a duty to make sure the care is arranged and that it is provided satisfactorily, but not as having a duty to do it himself.

These kinds of expectations, so widely held, totally ignore the changing role of women over recent years. A fantasy persists that all married women have a husband to support them and are at home doing the housekeeping. Taking on the care of an elderly or handicapped relative is thus seen as presenting a relatively small change in their life-style, an extra piece of responsibility which they take on gladly.

This, of course, is very far from the truth. Most married women have some kind of job — in the United Kingdom probably as many as 75 per cent — and when they become carers many of them try to continue working, thus finding themselves with a huge extra task.

There are particular problems for carers who are trying to hold down a job as well as taking full responsibility for the caring role.

My husband is dying of cancer, and after I've been all night without sleep because of looking after him, then have to go to work, the strain is terrific and I've made myself ill.

At the worst time I wasn't sure if I could keep on with my job. I collapsed once while I was teaching, after I had come home the previous evening to find mother hallucinating and telling me about the rats coming through the walls.

Another important feature about caring is that it is rarely shared. In fact, shared care between members of a family appears to be as rare as care which is shared between family carers and the statutory services. This is often a source of bitterness.

In 1981, my mother suffered a very severe stroke which took her right side and her speech. When she came out of hospital she couldn't do anything and I used to go down to their house and help out. When she'd been home for about seven weeks my father died very suddenly. The night he died, my two elder brothers were there together with my husband and their two wives. We went upstairs to another room to discuss what was to be done about mother and all I got was complete silence. They just did not want to know. So I said I would have her. My husband did not particularly want her, but I insisted she was not going into a home. I asked both my brothers to help out at weekends, but one only did it once and never offered again, while the other would have her one Sunday a month between 11.30 a.m. and 3.30 p.m. Even when I had to go into hospital to have a lump removed from my breast, they wouldn't help. My two boys moved in together to make room for Mum, and then she suggested that she would give us some money to have a loft conversion. We did this and it made life a lot easier as the boys could then have their own rooms.

Mum was with us for five years, and in that time was very happy and contented and recovered most of her speech. Fourteen months before she died she gave us £1,000 to thank us for looking after her so well. I got very depressed while I was caring for her, but I miss her terribly now. But the worst thing of all is that my brothers have accused us of robbing mother and we are facing a court case. Life is a living hell for me and I can't believe my brothers could behave like this when I looked after Mum for so long and they never even visited her on her birthday.

Young Carers

It has only come to light very recently that in certain family situations, very young people, even small children, are expected to take on the caring role. This usually occurs when a parent has a progressive illness, and develops gradually. At first, the child may only be expected to make a hot drink or to collect a prescription. Later, as the child develops competence, he or she becomes more and more essential to the sick parent, especially where there is a breakdown of the marriage, which often follows when one partner develops say, multiple sclerosis. Once the husband leaves, more and more responsibility falls on the child, until she may find herself washing and dressing a parent before school, rushing home at lunchtime to prepare food or take the parent to the lavatory, as well as taking responsibility for the rest of the household. The effect on the child's schooling and emotional development is dramatic. Meanwhile, the only solution which may be offered is to take the child into care and the parent into residential care. This stark choice will often lead to the sick parent colluding in a situation he or she knows to be unfair on the child, for fear of the consequences of bringing it to anyone's attention.

How long does it go on for?

The length of time that people spend as carers is immensely variable. It may be a few weeks only, or it can go on for many years — perhaps for as many as thirty. People are known to have spent thirty or more years caring for one person, or, like the woman in the following example, even longer caring for a series of people.

When I met my husband in 1933, his Dad was ill and I gave up my job to look after him until he died just before the war. When my children were growing up I looked after my own mother after she'd had a stroke. When my husband was 50, he got Parkinson's Disease and I looked after him for twelve years. I had to do everything for him for about eight years — bath him, shave him, feed him. Just after he died, in 1972, my daughter had breast cancer and I nursed her for three years. I suppose you could say I've been a carer all my life.

Caring may be intermittent —interspersed with periods in residential care, perhaps, or, more rarely, shared with someone else. It usually ends either with the death of the dependent person, or with his or her admission to some kind of residential care, because the carer is simply unable to continue with the task any longer.

What does a Carer do?

Physical Tasks

Much of caring is about hard, physical work. The more disabled the person you are caring for, the harder will be your tasks. You will probably have to get involved in heavy lifting, in toileting, in washing, dressing and changing soiled clothes and underwear, in feeding, perhaps in administering medication. Some carers perform tasks which might be expected to be more properly performed by medical or nursing staff, such as setting a catheter or giving an injection, or manually evacuating the bowels.

A typical day for a carer looking after her husband who has had a severe stroke is described by this woman:

In the morning I lift my husband from the bed onto a chair, and then I help him to a standing position and help him to the bathroom where I give him a good wash-down from head to foot, especially if he has wet himself in the night. I just can't get him into the bath. Then I bring him downstairs. He can only descend backwards and I do the same, making sure he doesn't miss his footing. Once downstairs I dress him and put him into his chair, where he has a special table that holds the newspaper which he likes to read. I give him his breakfast and sometimes, just as he is about to have it, he wants to pass water and for this we have a bottle.

About an hour after breakfast he usually wants to go to the toilet to open his bowels, so it's back upstairs again. He doesn't always make it to the toilet and then I have to clean him up, but I just can't face the thought of having a commode downstairs. When we are down again, I give him his electric razor and he tries to have a shave. By now it's time for coffee, so I sit with him and have one.

Then I go back upstairs and change the bed and put the sheets in the machine. My daughter bought me a tumble dryer recently, and it's such a boon. Then I do a bit of housework, all the time checking on him to see he's all right. I never leave him to go out shopping as I'm too nervous and he gets very weepy if I do, so I go shopping when he is at the stroke club on a Thursday, and apart from that just manage with what the milkman can supply.

About noon I start getting the dinner. He enjoys his food, and that's the best time of day, really. It's not all bad, because sometimes we have a laugh while we are eating. Then he sleeps while I wash up and do some more housework or cooking. I try to listen to 'Woman's Hour', because the people on it seem like friends to me and I don't really have anyone call at the house any more. But most likely he'll wake up in the middle of it and we have a cup of tea. In the summer, if the weather is warm, I manage with great difficulty to get him down the steps and into his wheelchair and then into the garden, which he enjoys.

I am a bundle of nerves in the early evening, because he went through a stage of having really bad convulsions at about this time. He had them for about two years but hasn't had one for a month now. We watch TV a bit in the evenings, but we can't talk much, really, and he cries a lot then, which I think is only to be expected in a person who one minute is hale and hearty and full of life, and then is struck down like this. It takes me about an hour to get him up to bed. He's in a single bed now and I sleep on a mattress on the floor, next to him. I try to read a bit, but I'm usually too tired, and I know he'll call me two or three times in the night.

It is perhaps not surprising that carers suffer great disturbance to their health as a result of their caring role. A survey carried out by the Equal Opportunities Commission in 1980 found that 21 per cent of the carers interviewed described their health as 'poor', and only 54 per cent felt it was 'good' or 'very good'; while a survey carried out by the Crossroads Care Scheme in 1983 found that 64 per cent of the carers they interviewed were in poor health. The data gathered from the 1985 General Household Survey showed that more than half the carers aged over 45 reported a long-standing illness.

Most carers are given no training for the necessary physical tasks. Somehow, they are expected to know by instinct what is required, in much the same way that women are expected to know automatically how to care for a baby. A colleague quotes the example of a child learning to swim: 'If we try to teach someone to swim, few people would do it by throwing them into the deep end with no instruction whatsoever. We give them arm bands, teach them the strokes and encourage them slowly. But carers are thrown into the deep end of caring with no knowledge and no skills and expected to cope.'

One carer I met, a man of about 60 who was caring for his severely disabled wife, put it like this:

When my wife was in hospital, it took four nurses to lift and turn her; now she's at home I have to do it all on my own. Is that what they call Community Care?

It is not surprising that many carers injure themselves.

The bed we had was so low and I didn't know how to lift him, so my back began to give me trouble. After a few weeks I slipped a disc.

But the job of caring involves much more than just physical tasks. The financial burden is severe.

Finances

In Chapter 2 will be found details of the help carers can get, but at present the financial support available simply does not take account of the commitment which many find it necessary to make.

A carer's ability to earn is affected by caring. She may have to take a job which pays badly, simply because it fits in with the demands made on her. Many have to give up paid work altogether, as it is impossible to fit it in with their caring duties. But loss of earnings is only one aspect of the financial cost to a family of caring for a dependent relative. The day-to-day living costs of a disabled person are often heavy, with heating, laundry and special food making his or her expenses considerably higher than those of an ordinary person. In addition, families may have to buy extra bedding, incontinence equipment, and also to buy in substitute care on occasions. In 1982 the Family Policies Studies Centre published figures about the cost of care given by informal carers, which estimated that the value to the National Exchequer was between five and seven billion pounds sterling a year.

The Emotional Burden

The stress involved in caring is certainly very great in terms of physical effort and finances. But undoubtedly most carers would say that their worst problems are of an emotional nature.

Carers feel isolated. They feel angry, resentful, embarrassed by the tasks they have to perform; they feel a sense of loss for the person who was once so close to them and is no longer. For many the strain is insupportable, and they suffer symptoms of stress, perhaps a complete breakdown. They may feel that the demands made on them, not only by the person they are caring for but by other members of their families, are intolerable.

It was all too much, but I only realised it when I'd just flipped my lid one night. For two years I'd been trying to balance out the needs of my mother, who was growing more and more demanding, with the needs of my family. I managed it when the kids were small, but when they started to grow up and be a bit ... well, not difficult ... but just like teenagers are, the scales just couldn't be balanced any more.

There is one emotion above all which carers suffer and seem unable to cope with: the feeling of guilt. Whatever they do, somehow it is never enough.

Why do they feel this guilt? It seems to be related to the enormously strong moral pressure society places on us to care for those relatives who need our help. It is, for example, remarkable how often phrases like 'for better or for worse', 'honour thy father and mother', 'suffer little children', are used by carers when they are questioned about why they are carers.

Even though we may know intellectually that caring for an elderly parent, a disabled spouse or a handicapped child is going to have a traumatic effect on our lives, there is still a strong moral imperative to do it. We shall be looking more at this in Chapter 3.

There is evidence to suggest that carers find the emotional problems of being a carer far more difficult to cope with than any others. It does not seem to be the heaviness of the tasks which causes the worst problems, but the nature of the relationship within which these tasks are carried out. Whilst an intimate and close emotional relationship with the person for whom you are caring may make it more difficult to perform the personal tasks which are necessary, it also makes you better able to cope with the emotional stress of caring:

The first time my mother messed the bed, I thought both she and I would die when I had to clean her up. But we managed and have gone on managing. I have always loved her dearly and respected her, too. She never tried to interfere in my life and has always trusted me and somehow or other managed to make me feel valued. Even when I married a man she didn't care for she made it absolutely clear that she respected my decision and did not try to influence me. So somehow now, I know we both have that respect for each other still and it gets us through the worst times.

The experience of another carer is very different:

I often lie to people and say that it's the caring, the grinding hard work and the mess, which has made my love for mother turn to dislike. But the truth is, she and I always disliked each other — at least I feel she disliked me when I was born because I wasn't a boy and I took the lead from her as I grew up. So now that I'm trapped into this caring business, I feel pretty resentful. It isn't easy to wash the soiled sheets of someone you dislike. Relationships don't

*change when you are a carer, they just get more like they were
before.*

How does Caring end?

There are many ways in which the role of carer can come to
an end. The person for whom you have been caring may
recover from the illness, for example, or move to the home
of another member of the family. The carer herself may
become ill, not an uncommon occurrence, and be unable to
continue. But it is most likely that the caring will come to an
end in one of two ways: the cared for person will either die
or go into some kind of residential care. Both situations are
difficult for the carer to cope with. The 'letting go' which is
involved in the move to residential care and the guilt feelings which accompany it, together with the particular problems of adjustment following bereavement, which carers
face, will be examined in Chapter 3.

2 What Help can Carers get?

I feel as though there is a great mushroom of information up there somewhere, and if I could only get into the stem of it I could find my way up and all sorts of things would be available to me, I would find all sorts of help. But how to get into the stem, that's the problem.

This is a familiar feeling for many carers. There is very little uniformity of service between one area of the country and another: what is available to carers living in one town may be unheard of by carers living in the next. So when we talk about services which are available to carers it is only possible to give a rough idea of what *may* be available, and encourage the carer to ask. Asking may not be easy since, as the carer above indicates, it may be almost impossible to find your way about the system. It is not the responsibility of any single person or department to give information to carers, and as a consequence many slip through the net. Even the most articulate and experienced find difficulty, and even people who have worked as professionals are often astonished at how difficult it becomes when they find themselves in the position of being the seeker of information, rather than the keeper of it. As one social worker put it:

I could not believe how difficult it was. I knew who to contact, I even knew the phone numbers of the various departments, but still I kept being shunted from one to the other, given conflicting opinions and generally messed around. What amazed me most of all was how unwilling I was to make a fuss or get stroppy. I realised I felt I had no right to the services and I was asking people for favours which somehow I had no right to.

These feelings are common among carers and no doubt spring from the thought that they *ought* to be able to manage without asking anyone for anything.

Help for carers is patchy and often inadequate, but there is a range of services which can make their lives infinitely more bearable, and people who act as gatekeepers to many other sources of help.

THE GENERAL PRACTITIONER (GP)

The family doctor is the first person the carer thinks about and one of the most important gatekeepers. He is the means by which most people get health care and can be crucial to whether carers receive help or not.

If you've got a good GP you're made.
Without my doctor I don't know where I'd be.

Of course, GPs are very variable, as the experience of this 70-year-old looking after her husband of 77 will illustrate.

My husband had a heart attack at home three years ago and another when he got to the hospital, but they pulled him through. The advice I was given was that he should rest and that we should get out of this house because he is not supposed to climb stairs and because we have an outside toilet. But we were turned down by the Council and didn't know what to do next. We decided to stick it out and I shouldered all the work. We paddled along together, not bothering anybody. Hubby would go for his check-up and tablets that he is on for life. Three months ago he fell and broke a few of his ribs and had to stay in bed, with me carrying bedpans. After that episode he had a second fall, this time injuring his groin. He was sent to the local hospital for X-rays, but neither our doctor nor anyone at the hospital asked how we were coping. But we were

*used to this attitude from doctors and didn't attach much impor-
tance to it.*

*However, just a month ago, hubby became worse and my left
arm was one big ache, so I had to send for the doctor. This time it
was a locum who wanted hubby X-rayed again. He diagnosed me
as having tennis elbow. Much to my astonishment, he asked me if I
was a carer, had I got the allowances and did I need a home help? To
me, as you can imagine, all this was amazing as I'd never heard
anything like it. However, a lady from social services came to see
us and the following week a home help came, and just this morning
I've had a man from the Council about re-housing us. I don't want
to seem miserable and discontented, but why didn't my own doctor
arrange these things when he's been seeing my hubby all this time?
I could have asked, I suppose, but we were managing to keep our
heads above water and keep our pride.*

Finding what a difference can be made by a different
doctor was also the experience of this woman, who is caring
for her mother and step-father.

*When they were complaining of all sorts of ailments, I never
knew whether to call the doctor or not. Once when I called him he
seemed very cross and said their problems were just old age and he
couldn't cure that! But about that time a rather young female GP
joined the practice, and I can never say enough good about her. She
has been an absolute angel and nothing is too much trouble. She
told me never to fear ringing for her to come out to visit Mum and
Dad at any time, and she has such marvellous patience. She
encourages me all the time and tells me what a marvellous job I'm
doing. She even arranged for them to go to a home for two weeks a
year while I have a holiday with my husband.*

Although it is not always necessary for the carer to go via
the GP to find her way to the professionals who can help
her, many services are dependent on a referral from a GP
and almost all are easier to come by with the GP's support.
Some carers have the same GP as the person they care for:
they feel it is more satisfactory if the doctor knows the
whole situation. Other carers feel that the doctor may pay

more attention to the needs of the person being cared for, to regard that person as the patient and the main focus of his attention, thereby neglecting the needs of the carer. It is sometimes better, carers feel, to have their own, separate GP, so that they can speak more frankly to the doctor about their problems.

Consultants

If the person being cared for is admitted to hospital or is referred to a hospital by the GP, the carer may get help and advice from a hospital consultant — from a paediatrician if the patient is a child, from a geriatrician if the patient is elderly, or from a psychiatrist or psychogeriatrician if the problem is a mental one. Some of these hospital-based specialists will do home visits, but most of them only operate from their hospital.

Other Health Workers

District Nurses have had special training in helping people at home. They will visit to administer drugs and change dressings. They may be able to offer training in how to lift someone or how to deal with incontinence, and can also provide the carer with a whole range of helpful equipment such as ripple beds, bath seats, incontinence pads and commodes, as well as extra help with bathing.

Health Visitors are nurses who have had special training in working with families at home. They once worked only with families with small children, but there are now many who work with elderly people. They do not undertake practical nursing tasks but focus more on the emotional side. Carers may be able to talk to them about the stress of caring and about any relationship difficulties. The Health Visitor will also be able to give advice about other local services, both statutory and voluntary, and can often advise about benefits.

Community Psychiatric Nurses (CPNS) have had special training in mental illness and can support families who are coping with this kind of problem. They will give information about drugs and can help the carer by giving advice on coping with difficult behaviour.

Continence Advisors can assess incontinence problems, treat or even cure incontinence, give practical advice on coping and provide special equipment such as pads and special clothing.

The task of the **Occupational Therapist (OT)** is to help an elderly or disabled person to cope with a disability and to help him or her manage such daily tasks as dressing or cooking. For example, when someone who has had a stroke is discharged from hospital, the OT will do a home visit with the patient, to see him in his own home and to assess not only whether he will be able to cope, but also whether any aids or adaptations will be necessary. These could include handrails, ramps or possibly a hoist.

Physiotherapists help patients become more mobile through exercise. They can do home visits to people with mobility problems. They can suggest play therapy, perhaps, for a handicapped child and may be able to help carers by teaching them to lift or move someone without injuring themselves.

Other health workers who may be available to help carers will include chiropodists, speech therapists, opticians and dentists. Again, their availability, and whether or not they can do home visits, will vary from area to area.

SOCIAL WORKERS

Social workers are employed by the Local Authority and, like GPs, can act as gatekeepers, enabling carers to gain access to a range of services. They may also be able to provide the carer with help and advice on a wide range of personal problems, as well as practical and financial ones. Some social workers (Medical Social Workers) are attached to hospitals, while others work from general practices or health centres. Social workers may be able to put carers in touch with any one of the following services.

Meals on Wheels
Most Local Authorities run a service which provides a hot meal in the middle of the day for people who find difficulty in cooking for themselves. They are delivered to the door, often by volunteers.

Home Helps
A Home Help does light cleaning work or shopping, and in some areas will undertake more personal care. They are sometimes called Home Care or Domiciliary Care or Home Aides. There is a severe shortage of Home Helps, and this means that they are usually placed with people who live alone rather than with homes in which there are carers. Most Local Authorities charge a fee for a Home Help, and recipients pay according to their means.

Care Attendants
These schemes provide help of various kinds to fit the needs of the carer and the person cared for. Essentially, they aim to take the place of the carer and are willing to undertake any of the tasks which the carer would normally do. They can sit with the dependent person, get him up in the morning, put him to bed or attend to his personal needs. Care Attendants are trained and paid, but the service is usually free to the carer, with the Local Authority footing the bill. These Care Attendant schemes go under various names, such as Crossroads Care, Family Support or Domiciliary Care schemes. They are much appreciated by carers because they are flexible and place an emphasis on doing exactly what the carer normally does.

I don't think it's an exaggeration to say that Crossroads has saved me. I don't get it very often, just once a week on a Wednesday. But the marvellous thing is that the attendant comes at four in the afternoon, gives Michael his tea, sits with him in the evening, does his toilet routine and puts him to bed. I go to the shops, then to the library, and then I either go to see a friend or in winter to an evening class. I've done Yoga and this year I'm doing French conversation. Just having that time on my own means I can cope the rest of the time. I used to have friends who would offer to sit with him, but it wasn't the same because I was always worried; whereas with Crossroads, even though it's not always the same lady, you know they are trained and will be able to cope even if he falls or something.

Carers are united in their praise for these Care Attendant schemes. As one said:

What I really need is a robot, exactly like me, to take my place for a couple of hours a day. My care attendant isn't a robot but she is as near as I can come to an exact replica of me.

Sitting Services

Another service which can help carers by providing someone to sit with the dependent person. Unlike Care Attendants, sitters are not usually trained, but they may well have had experience of caring. They are sometimes run by Local Authorities or Health Authorities, but they are also often run by voluntary groups and some carers groups set up their own Sitting Services. Sitters will 'mind' the dependent person for a few hours during the day or evening.

Aids and Adaptations

Adaptations can be made to homes to enable carers and cared-for people to cope better. Handrails can be fitted, ramps installed, hoists put in above baths or beds. As well as these major items there is a huge range of pieces of equipment which can help people dress, use the lavatory, cook or reach things.

Laundry Service

For those caring for someone who is incontinent, bed linen can be laundered and sometimes clothing too. There is often a small charge.

I didn't know about the incontinence service till I went to the carers group and someone there mentioned it. I suppose they worry

that too many people will want it if they publicise it, because it is
such a boon to those of us with handicapped children and no doubt
for those with elderly folk, too.

TRANSPORT SERVICES

Most Local Authorities offer reduced or free fares to disabled, handicapped and elderly people. Many also offer
community transport schemes of various kinds, which may
be able to provide door-to-door transport in specially converted vehicles with tail lifts. These are often referred to as
'Dial a Ride' schemes. Availability and charges vary
greatly, as does the type of person who can be transported.
Health Authorities will usually provide free transport to
Day Hospitals, hospitals and clinics. Transport to Day
Centres may also be free, but in some places a charge is
made.

Adaptations to privately owned vehicles may be available also, and there is a range of help for disabled drivers,
such as parking concessions and stickers.

VOLUNTARY SERVICES

All the above services may be provided through a Local
Authority, but there is also a wide range of voluntary services which may be useful to carers. It is even more difficult
to indicate exactly what will be available from the voluntary
sector, because by its very nature it tends to be patchy,
organised at a very local level, and services tend to spring
up quite suddenly in response to need. Each local area will
have its own network of voluntary services which can help
and support carers and their dependants. Each network
will be different and the amount of support available will
vary from place to place. There may be a volunteer co-
ordinator at the hospital or the social services department,
who can direct carers to services.

Many towns will have a Council of Voluntary Service

(CVS) which acts as a co-ordinating body for the voluntary sector, and more rural areas will have a Community Council which performs the same function. Both these Councils will be in close contact with voluntary organisations. Many areas will have a Volunteer Bureau which can put those needing voluntary service in touch with those who are willing to give it. There are of course voluntary organisations which have carers as their specific focus. There are two National ones: Carers National Association for anyone whose life is in some way restricted by the need to look after someone else, and Contact-a-Family which runs local support groups for the parents of children with special needs and a phone-in contact line.

INTERPRETERS

We live in a multi-cultural society, and some Local Authorities or voluntary services recognise this by providing interpreters for carers, who can help to translate documents or explain services to those for whom English may not be a first language.

* * *

So far I have concentrated on help which can be given to help the carer and the dependant in the home. Some of this, like Care Attendant schemes, enables carers to get away for a short time, and this is what many carers say they need. 'Time off' or 'Time to be me' is a very valued part of the help available to carers.

RESPITE CARE

Most of us expect to have holidays, to have the weekend off, to have a lunch hour. No one any longer expects people to work a 16-hour day or to work at Christmas. But carers have no agreed working week and no recognised time off.

It is the non-stop nature of the work, the feeling that you can **never** get away, that leads carers to feel completely trapped; so relief care, where the dependent person is looked after for a week, two weeks, a day, or part of a day, can be, as one carer put it, 'a life saver'.

It is important to remember that the fact that the following forms of respite care *can* be found does not mean that they *will* be found. Again, the situation is immensely variable.

A Stay in Hospital

Some general hospitals and almost all mental handicap, psychiatric and geriatric hospitals keep some special beds which can be used to admit a dependent person to respite care so that the carer can have a break. There is great variation in how they are organised. Some will arrange admission once a year for two weeks, so that the carer can go away on holiday. Others prefer to offer shorter, more frequent admissions. In some areas, with a very heavily dependent person, the carer is offered a 'shared care scheme', so that the cared-for person spends, say, two weeks at home, followed by two weeks in hospital, followed by another two weeks at home, and so on. Such schemes have their pros and cons as far as carers are concerned.

The hospital may be situated a long way from the carer's home, and many hospitals are rather more geared to nursing the sick than to providing loving care for the disabled or elderly. In addition, a mentally disabled child or a confused elderly person may be very disorientated by leaving home and in need of more individual attention than is often possible in a busy hospital ward. On the other hand, many carers find that this sort of planned admission fits in well with their lives and with the needs of the person they are caring for. Sometimes a stay in hospital will enable the dependent person to receive treatment, assessment or therapy to which they would not normally have access.

It took me ages to agree to letting John go into hospital so that his father and I could have a break. In fact it was only when my husband said he would go on holiday without me if I wouldn't go with him that I agreed to give it a try. It was terrible to leave him there — I felt so guilty. But when we came back he had had a lovely time and was much better. He'd been seen by the consultant who had prescribed some new drugs for his fits, and also the speech therapist. His speech is so much better now and I'm taking him for follow-up treatment every month. I was so pleased about this respite scheme that when I heard it might be stopped because of the cuts, I joined a protest group, and though I've never done anything like it before, I've been speaking to groups of people and getting a petition signed.

A Stay in a Nursing Home or Residential Home

Though these establishments are usually for permanent care, many have a few places available for short-term placements. In nursing homes, special care is provided by qualified nursing staff, while residential homes provide general care and supervision but not nursing care. Local Authority homes will be free to the carer, but private establishments charge fees which are very variable, although sometimes the carer can get help towards these. The standard of both nursing and residential homes is very variable also, although they do have to be registered with either the local Council or the Health Authority.

Short Term Foster Care

Many Local Authorities have been successful in setting up schemes whereby foster parents are recruited and trained to look after mentally or physically disabled children while their parents have a holiday. The schemes are very well received by those who take advantage of them. The real parents are usually encouraged to meet the prospective foster parents and discuss the care which is needed. The schemes are normally free to parents, but they are increasingly available too for elderly dependants, when a small fee may be charged. Even quite severely confused elderly people have been successfully 'fostered'. When Anne went to see the family home into which her mother was to go she had misgivings.

It wasn't that I thought the home wasn't nice enough or anything like that — on the contrary, I thought it was all too immaculate and that they wouldn't be able to cope with mother's incontinence. I was very embarrassed to mention it, but when I did, the family couldn't have been nicer. They were very matter-of-fact about it and showed me all the equipment they had. It was very reassuring.

Holidays

Sometimes it is possible to arrange a holiday for the dependant at a home which caters especially for such people. This will enable the carer to go away on a holiday of her own or, perhaps even better for the carer, to stay at home and do her own thing for a week or a fortnight. Holidays can be arranged too, which enable the carer and the dependant to go away together, but to a home or hotel where the carer is relieved of day-to-day tasks. Some Local Authorities arrange these holidays, but they are more usually arranged by various voluntary organisations, such as the Parkinson's Disease Society or the Chest, Heart and Stroke Association. The Holiday Care Service and the Royal Association for Disability and Rehabilitation (Radar) provide information and advice services.

Day Care

Sometimes the carer does not want relief for a week or two at a stretch, but for an hour or a few hours each day, or a couple of days each week. Day Hospitals, Day Centres and Lunch Clubs are the three types of care usually available.

Day Hospitals are for people who require regular medical treatment or specialised care. Doctors, nurses and social workers are usually present, and often other health professionals, such as physiotherapists or chiropodists, are available. Patients usually attend for a limited period, or for a period which is regularly reviewed. They are free of charge, and transport is generally provided to and from the Day Hospital.

Day Centres have a recreational, not a medical focus. Some undertake rehabilitation of patients, from a stroke, say; others teach skills but many concentrate on craftwork, games and group activities. It would be a rare Day Centre which did not have an occasional bingo session! A hot meal is usually provided, for which there may be a charge. They are staffed by both professionals and volunteers and organised by Local Authorities and many voluntary groups. Transport is often provided, again possibly at a cost, but there are frequent complaints about the unreliability of transport, especially the fact that it may come at any time between 9 a.m. and 11 a.m. to pick up someone who has been waiting for more than two hours.

Lunch or Social Clubs are usually very locally based, run by volunteers and often grouped around a particular interest, religion or culture. A charge is usually made for lunch and transport is not normally available.

OTHER KINDS OF SUPPORT

Most of the help offered to carers is of a practical nature, but as will be apparent from some carers' situations, one of the most important forms of support which can be offered is emotional support. The opportunity to 'talk to someone who understands' is something which many carers consider a 'life-saver', and counselling may be available to them in some, though by no means all, areas.

Counselling
Coming to terms with the feelings involved in caring is difficult and, for some carers, may be impossible.

I didn't mind the incontinence or even the confusion so much — it was when she didn't know me and then was so aggressive to me; that used to make me feel a wreck.

Talking things over in confidence with someone who is outside the situation can be very reassuring for a carer. People do find it very difficult to discuss their true feelings, especially if those feelings are of anger or something else which they feel is in some way unacceptable. Social workers sometimes perform this role for carers, as do some other specialist agencies such as the Samaritans or the Marriage Guidance Council — now called Relate. However, it is much more likely that carers will receive this kind of emotional support from some kind of carers support group.

Carers Groups

In recent years there has been a rapid growth in self-help groups of all kinds, and carers groups are a particularly effective body. Some groups are very local, while some are adjuncts or branches of national associations. They undertake a range of tasks — they may provide information or be merely social.

There is a huge range, in terms both of style and of participant. Some are started by a social worker or other professional; some are run largely by carers themselves; some will have a campaigning, 'doing' style, with an emphasis on getting things done, others will pay far more attention to enabling carers to meet each other and share their problems. Still others will be interested in providing services to other carers to help them cope — such as a sitting service, for example. Some groups will place the emphasis on outings and social activities which will enable carers to forget their problems for the time being. Carers groups mean different things to different people, like any other groups, and they are certainly not helpful to everybody, but to those who try them they can be very supportive. The following carers had different experiences of carers groups.

I knew the Health Visitor had started this group in our area because she never failed to mention it every time she came to see me. In fact I got a bit sick of her mentioning this parents' group because I had told her I'd never been a joiner and didn't want to sit around moaning with a lot of other parents of handicapped children. But I suppose eventually I got tired of saying no and this particular meeting was fixed to coincide with a session in the clinic for the children, so I decided to pop in. At first it was just as I had feared, and there was no way I was going to speak because I felt it would be disloyal to Joseph. After a bit this one parent — actually it was a father — started to talk about his daughter and her sleeping habits, and it was as if he'd switched on a light — it was Joseph to a tee. I still didn't say anything, but I listened to the reactions of the others and especially to one woman who'd solved the problems by a particular routine before bedtime. I didn't say anything at all that first time, except thank you for a cup of tea, but I tried this routine with Joseph and it worked! I went back to the group the next week and told them about it. It seemed as if they were my friends, as if they knew what the problems of looking after a handicapped child were, in a way that no one else had ever done. I wouldn't miss my Tuesday afternoon now for anything. We find we can always help each other in some way, even if it's only offering a shoulder to cry on.

I saw this advert in the paper, asking for people who were interested in joining a carers group, and something clicked. I was caring for both my parents-in-law at the time and feeling pretty het up about it. I had had to give up a good job and I was just so angry, even though I knew it was the right thing to do. When I went to the first meeting they needed someone to be secretary, and somehow I found myself volunteering. I must say that I have never looked back. A few months later the social worker who had started the group left to have a baby and I found myself as the Chairman. Then I was asked to give an interview to the local paper and then to do a broadcast on Radio Essex. I seem to have found myself being the voice for carers, and I sit on all sorts of committees and planning groups now. My father-in-law died last year and my mother-in-law had to go into a home finally last autumn, but caring issues are still high on my agenda. In fact, I really feel that I've found some sort of new career, or at least a life-long interest, through it.

FINANCIAL SUPPORT

Apart from the practical and emotional support available to carers, there is a series of benefits to which both carers and dependants have a right.

It is not appropriate here to provide a comprehensive list, but there are three main benefits about which no carer should be ignorant.

Attendance Allowance
This is paid to anyone over two years of age who needs help with eating, drinking, using the toilet, dressing, etc., and who has been in need of such help for the previous six months. There are two rates, the lower one for day *or* night attendance, the higher one for day *and* night attendance. It can be paid to anyone, regardless of age or income. It is not means tested and not taxed.

Mobility Allowance
This can be claimed by anyone between the ages of 5 and 66 who is unable or virtually unable to walk. It is tax free and not means tested, but it stops at the age of 75.

Invalid Care Allowance
This is the only benefit which is payable directly to carers, and is for anyone who has given up work to look after someone and is doing so for at least 35 hours per week. The person being looked after has to be claiming attendance allowance, and the claimant must be aged between 16 and 60 if female, or 16 and 65 if male. ICA is taxable and is counted in with other benefits when assessments are made.

In addition to these benefits, carers on low incomes will also be entitled to a range of other benefits via the income support system. They may also be able to get free prescriptions, exemption from road tax, parking concessions and, until the Community Charge is introduced, some rate relief.

Though all the above and sometimes some other benefits *should* be available to carers, they are often ignorant of them, and even when they know about them, very reluctant to claim. As always, it comes back to the strong moral pressure which makes carers feel that it is their duty to care and that they have no *right* to any benefits or to any help.

Citizens' Advice Bureaux and other advice centres can be very helpful to carers, to explain what their entitlements are and to help them make claims. More than one in six claimants consult these agencies, but in spite of that there is a huge lack of take-up of benefits — estimated in 1983–84 to be as much as £600 million, and no doubt much greater now because of the introduction in April 1988 of a new system of Social Security benefits. In any event, the financial help available to carers is completely inadequate and in urgent need of review. This will be discussed in greater detail in Chapter 7.

At the beginning of this chapter, I quoted a carer who spoke about a 'mushroom' of information about the help which might be available. From what I have said in this chapter, it should be apparent that the range of help which *may* be available to a carer is wide. But no one should make the mistake of assuming that because it may be available, carers actually receive it. The census data published in 1988 revealed that 1.7 million carers live in the same household as the cared-for person. Of these, two thirds (66 per cent) receive no regular visits at all from health services, social services or voluntary groups.

3 The Emotions

'It's no use, unless you've experienced it you can't know what on earth it's going to be like,' is something which carers often say. Of course, you could say the same about most human situations which are filled with personal distress. What person who has not experienced it could imagine the pain of divorce, or of a bereavement, for example? Perhaps the only difference with caring is that more people imagine they know what it is like. I have said that caring always takes place within the context of a relationship, and perhaps it is for that reason that those who take it on *believe* they are going to know what to expect.

Because caring can be such a distressing experience it is tempting to begin any account of what carers feel with a long list of these distresses, but we would do well to remember that caring can bring joy, too, and it can certainly bring happiness in helping carers feel they are fulfilling a duty or returning love given to them in the past, or even in just fulfilling an obligation.

Just now and again, you know, we have a laugh about things, or there is just a flash of his old wit. Then I think how lucky I am that I've still got him here with me — not like some of my friends who are already widows.

It may sound a bit odd to you but we still find some fun between us. Its usually when we remember some funny incident from the past — something she said — or remembering with affection someone who is now dead.

There are times, you know, which seem to make it all worthwhile — make me even thankful she's as she is — does that sound wicked? What I mean is, it sometimes makes me happy that she won't grow up and grow away from me. Say it's a winter afternoon, snowing, perhaps, and all the lights just coming on. I remember when my other children were at home and on an afternoon like that we'd settle down to watch the TV and maybe toast crumpets. I can remember feeling almost a physical pain because I knew those precious moments were limited and would pass. With Elaine, they won't pass, she'll always be with me, always need me. Those cosy moments are worth a lot. Usually I envy other mothers because they have children who aren't handicapped. On those winter afternoons I wouldn't change places with any one of them.

These joyful experiences seem to be rare though. More frequently carers say:

Caring has made me a physical and mental wreck, totally unable to relax and without a clue how to even try to think of myself.

What is it about caring which makes people 'emotional wrecks'? For a start, there is the huge mixture of emotions which it involves.

My emotions seemed to be mixed. It was dreadful to see mother suffer and know there was nothing more to be done to help her, but I sometimes felt guiltily sceptical when she complained of nausea just before I had to leave for a late shift, which she hated, or if she began vomiting when I was about to take a rare holiday. There was frustration when I found she had arranged for me to entertain another elderly relative when I had been looking forward to a week's leave to catch up with myself. There was fear as I saw myself getting older, her needs increasing and her demands on me getting greater. There was anger at the hopeless life I was living and there was hurt that, after all I had and all I had lost and given up for her, nothing would ever satisfy my mother. I was alone with my worries, my anger, my fears and my restricted lifestyle.

Clearly, carers are individuals and their emotions are their own. It could be construed as demeaning to talk about 'the emotions which carers feel'. Nonetheless, there are certain emotions which appear to be common to most carers.

ISOLATION

The feeling that no one cares about you *ever* is frequently mentioned.

My husband isn't fond of people coming to the house, he seems on edge. Friends we once had we do not see any more. In the past I have rung them, but they don't ring back any more. Some days I could put my coat on and walk out. My family do not seem to care. The worst time is Bank Holidays and Christmas. My daughter in Somerset comes up every other year, but other than that I get no Happy Birthday or Merry Christmas as every day is the same. My tears are reserved for my bath or shower when no one can see.

You get so dreadfully lonely, no one wants to know you and you are isolated. Say you go into a pub now and again, you have to rush back after an hour, so after a while you have no friends who go out with you. We have no friends who come to visit now. I myself get very lonely, though my husband plays squash every Friday, which I am glad about. This has been the hardest thing of all to accept, that no one wants to bother with us now. They don't mean to be unkind, but as we are only in our thirties one cannot hope for people of that age group to fall in with us.

Why does this happen? Why is it that people feel so left out, and indeed *are* left out by their friends? This is, of course, a similar experience to that of other people in a stressed situation, say being widowed or losing a child.

One explanation is that people are afraid of the emotions that may be revealed. 'I didn't mention it, I didn't want to upset her,' is a common statement when people are describing how they reacted to a widow, although clearly, the death is the one thing the widow needs to talk about. So it is themselves, their own feelings, they are trying to protect.

Perhaps, though, there are other reasons why carers are avoided. One is the helplessness which observers feel, the reminder of their own total inability to help the carer, however much they might wish to. Certainly this is a feeling common to professionals, as we shall see in Chapter 5.

Another reason is well expressed by a carer:

You see the thing is, everybody is terrified that it is going to happen to them, that they are going to find themselves in the same position before their time is up. They just don't want to have to think about it until they have to. I always used to see it in their eyes — they'd start thinking, 'Christ what is going to happen when my Mum gets old?' or 'Could I cope if my Fred got as helpless as her husband?'

This may very well be a correct interpretation, especially when, in these days of people living so much longer, most people can identify a member of their family who is likely to need care at some time in the future. People probably feel this less about dependants who are disabled. Though many people speculate about and fear the death of a loved one, few are able to conceptualise about caring for a disabled spouse, still less about the prospect of having a handicapped child.

You'd think it wouldn't be so hard to face, what with us having a handicapped person in the family, but you'd never believe the stick I got when I tried to make our Joan face the fact that she might have a child that was less than perfect. I was accused of being an alarmist, of wishing bad luck on the family, and God knows what else.

BEING UNDERVALUED

It hurts me when I think how I'm taken for granted. I'm not a wife in any sense of the word, I'm simply an overworked housekeeper. It is very much a man's world as far as I'm concerned. I have no status whatsoever. I hope I don't sound like a terrible wet blanket, but when no one values you it makes you feel and believe that you have no value at all.

A carer who was until very recently a consultant anaesthetist, enjoying great status in his professional life, said:

What hurts you most of all is that you appear to be become suddenly a person whose opinions count for absolutely nothing. I mean, there I was, someone who had had peoples' lives in my hands when they were on the operating table. Then, suddenly, no one believes what you are saying. I used to tell my sons how bad their mother was getting: you know, I'd tell them about the wandering and about the incontinence. I could see them exchanging glances of disbelief. I could imagine them saying to each other, 'The old boy is losing his marbles,' and so on — me, who'd been used to respect, even to deference, in my previous life. And the really awful thing about it is that I recognise that I've done precisely the same to patients without realising what I was doing.

Why are carers undervalued? Is it because we value people by their jobs and caring is not recognised as a job? Why are we resistant to seeing their needs? Is it that we cannot allow ourselves to recognise the needs of carers unless we can in some way meet them, because this makes us feel so inadequate?

FEAR

The carer who had been a consultant also discussed this emotion which carers frequently feel.

I simply couldn't bear to think of what would happen to her if I had an accident or a heart attack. I lived in constant fear of not being able to cope, and anxiety about what would happen if I couldn't.

Fear such as this is common, too, among the parents of mentally handicapped children.

What on earth is going to happen when we are dead and gone? No one will do what we have done, put up with his tantrums and that. You couldn't expect anyone else to take it on. Last year my wife had a heart attack and I swear the reason she recovered so quick was sheer blue funk about what would happen to Roger if she died.

RESENTMENT

I am a resentful, frustrated landlady keeping alive a tenant who once was my husband. My husband is totally apathetic and I have no interest in him as a person. I am doing my duty under protest because I can't do anything else. Our marriage ceased 17 years ago and I have no social contacts now. My children (who live in other parts of the country) I see only on rare occasions and my grandchildren are growing up without me. My daughters are married with their own families to care for and they are horrified at my position. I feel life has dealt me a bitter blow but I am powerless to change it. Is there an answer? We could face life like this for another 20 years — what a prospect!

My mother has always influenced and dominated my life. We were a one-parent family long before this became fashionable behaviour and I am sure the traumatic effect of my mother's brief marriage had its impact on my childhood. Anyway, I was considered too shy and sensitive to mix with others in the normal way, so much so that I was completely unprepared to go out to work and so I stayed at home and became a housewife when I left school and my grandmother died. My mother has always felt I should be grateful for my sheltered life and I was quite satisfied with it, despite the privations, as we were always very short of money. Everything we had went into buying a house which became the most important thing in our lives, as we hoped to be able to take in lodgers and thus to make a little money.

Things did not work out. We have made a bare living and have not been able to finish paying for the house or to keep up with the maintenance. Before she became so ill, I was going to insist that we leave, sell the house and go our separate ways. But of course when you think of it that's a pipe dream. I've no experience, no money, no qualifications, no nothing, except a life-time of caring for a querulous old woman — who wants that?

When you feel your life has been so soured, it is natural to feel resentment, although sometimes carers find it impossible to admit this, even in an extreme case like this one:

As a child I was given to my grandmother to be brought up — evidently my mother never wanted children. I bear no ill feelings about that situation as my gran gave me a wonderful childhood,

*full of love and learning. I do not look after Mum now because I
have to but because I want to. I am doing for her what she refused to
do for me.*

ANGER

*When I see him sitting there sometimes, it galls me so much, never
a thought of thanking me goes through his head. I want to scream
at him — 'How do you think you'd manage without me, you
helpless individual?'*

*Will I still be doing this when I'm 70 years old? Doesn't
anybody care?*

Carers can be angry at their situation, feeling trapped in a
role they did not seek and from which there is no escape.
They can be angry at the services — either at an individual
worker or at THEM for not providing what is so badly
needed. They can, of course, also be angry with the person
cared for, because THEY are the cause of all the trouble.
Frequently, they are angry with themselves, either for
getting into the situation in the first place, or simply for
being angry when they know it is really no one's fault —
particularly if they are angry with the dependant whose
fault they feel it can't be.
Sometimes, perhaps more frequently than many of us
would like to admit, that anger inevitably leads to physical
abuse — always a source of anxiety and pain for the carer.

*At home the pressures continued, and I found it more and more
difficult to remain calm. I would shout at her and smack her when
she would not let me rest.*

*Look, I don't believe in smacking any child, let alone a handi-
capped child, but you want to try living with one. I defy anybody to
do it without getting to the pitch of hitting them now and again —
it's just more than flesh and blood could stand.*

*I never did hit him, but I have to admit giving him a push
sometimes. I'm careful, I only do it when there is something for*

him to fall onto, but if you've been cleaning up his mess and he laughs or just does it again, actually does it on you as you are cleaning him up — well, I'm human, after all.

GUILT

There is no doubt that of all the emotions, this is the most common among carers. Somehow, whatever you do, you feel it is not enough.

No doubt this results mostly from the strong moral pressure which exists in our society to provide care for other family members. This feeling of guilt seems to be inherent in most carers and surely comes from the complex set of notions about rights and responsibilities which most of us learn at a very early stage of our lives.

The feelings of guilt may be fostered by the person being looked after:

There is much resistance from my mother-in-law to any break away from home, which gives us a guilt complex if we say we need to get away. The prior preparations in arranging for sufficient food and for attendance and attention during the period we are away detracts considerably from the pleasure of occasionally getting away for a few days.

Frankly, the main thing you need is time away, but you know what happens, you know the things they say:

'Don't worry about me' — meaning and indicating, 'I shall probably drop dead while you are away but you go and enjoy yourself, you heartless thing.' Or, 'If you think it will help you, I'll go and stay in that place beside the sea' — meaning, 'I shall have to be uprooted, it'll be dirty, I'll hate the place, the food and everyone there and I may drop dead — but of course YOU need the break, dear.'

Even if you want to pop out to the shops in the morning, you watch the clock, delay the coffee, then it's, 'You will be back for lunch? But don't worry about me, don't rush (but I may be dead, injured, starving, etc).'

Feelings of guilt may make it very difficult for carers to

accept any form of help for themselves. Because they feel that they ought to be coping and that they have somehow failed in their duty if they cannot, they often express the view that they could not even think about help for themselves.

However bad it is for me looking after him, it can't be as bad as it is for him, suffering from this awful disease (Alzheimer's). So I must just grit my teeth and see it through. I couldn't cope with the remorse I'd feel if I put him in a Day Centre even for a day, let alone in a home or something like that.'

Feelings of guilt may persist after the death of the cared-for person too:

Since she died I've been in an agony of remorse. I did shout at her sometimes, I just couldn't help it. But recently I saw this programme on TV about stroke victims and I realise now I didn't understand how bad it was for her and that maybe she didn't mean to be awkward — she just couldn't help it. I did try to understand but I know now that I didn't realise how bad it was and thought too much about myself.

EMBARRASSMENT

Imagine what it's like having friends round for a meal and having your mother walk naked into the room, demanding breakfast. Imagine having your husband tell your neighbour that you are starving him and trying to take all his money. Imagine taking your handicapped son to the local library and seeing him start to masturbate publicly. These kind of incidents are common for some carers. Even with less dramatic examples, the opportunities for embarrassment are frequent.

It is when the youngsters are around that you feel it most. You know, the smell and that. However much you spray and so on and in spite of spending a fortune on cleaning materials, you can never really get rid of the smell of incontinence.

I felt very sad when Mum's family made excuses not to visit her — I knew they were embarrassed when she made strange remarks and told them about the flocks of sheep in the house, or about the little king who visited her every day. They tried to tell me there was nothing wrong with her and that she was just a bit confused. I suppose they were trying to convince themselves.

It is not only the behaviour of the dependent person which can cause embarrassment to the carer. The intimate caring tasks which are necessary can be a source of great distress also. This is not usually the case with marital relationships, or in relationships with a child, but is very much the case with tasks done for parents.

My father had always been the most fastidious and private man, and the first time I had to bath him, I thought we would both die of shame. I steadfastly tried to wash his lower regions while chatting away and looking anywhere but at him, but I tell you honestly it was one time that I wished his mind had gone and that he didn't have all his wits about him.

I had never seen my mother in her underwear even — we weren't like some families who walk about half undressed. When I had to help dress her, I could feel her intense embarrassment and it was terrible. After a bit you get used to it, I suppose, but it isn't right — I shouldn't have had to do that and she shouldn't have had to put up with it. I tried to make her feel better by reminding her that she'd changed my nappies when I was a baby, but it doesn't really help. Somehow it's all right for a parent to have to do that for a child, but not the other way about.

ROLE REVERSAL

Having to act in a parental way to the person who once parented you causes enormous distress to carers. They find this reversal of roles one of the most difficult adjustments to make, cutting as it does across some of our most deeply held inhibitions and taboos. Most parent/child relationships do not easily allow intimate nursing tasks to be carried out without shame on the part of the recipient or embarrassment on the part of the performer.

Similarly, difficulties can arise when a wife is looking after a highly dependent husband (or, of course, though less frequently, vice versa). The normal marriage relationship is no longer possible and the spouse gradually takes on a new and unfamiliar role — that of parent.

I can't begin to describe what it's like to have to clean him up when he messes himself, but funnily enough even that isn't as bad as the fact that he can't take any of the decisions any more. I was just a little woman, you know, and he was such a lovely man — looked after me in every way — well, too much, really, though I didn't think so at the time. I couldn't even write a cheque, let alone decide which decorator we should have or when the car should be serviced. Now I have to do all that and I know it must hurt him. The worst thing was when I had to do all the arranging for my mother's funeral, when before he got Parkinson's he'd have done all that. We both put a brave face on but I can't bear it sometimes.

Sense of Loss

Carers often mourn the loss of the person who, as they put it, is 'no longer there'. The sense of loss they feel for that person who has gone is often acute. This is particularly true in situations where the illness or disability causes a complete change in temperament or disposition.

You see, he used to be so easy-going and lovable, the sweetest chap; now he's different again — moody, bad-tempered, inconsiderate. Sometimes I look at him and think, 'God, Tom, where did you go to?'

This sense of loss can be acute, even when the carer and the cared-for person have not been especially close.

I can't say mother and I were particularly intimate, but I always knew where I was with her. She called a spade a spade and you more or less knew how she'd react. What I find so hard now is never

*knowing how she's going to be. I open the bedroom door in a
morning and I never know which of a dozen different people is
going to confront me.*

THE EFFECTS OF EMOTIONAL STRESS

It has been estimated that 58 per cent of full-time carers are
suffering from the effects of emotional stress. In some studies, as many as half of those considered have been found to
be at risk of psychiatric illness. Some of them suffer a
complete emotional breakdown, others exist on tranquillisers. The majority manage to carry on somehow, often at the
expense of their own future mental health. Everyone needs
to be able to use some of their own personal energy on
themselves, in order to renew the energy they expend
elsewhere; carers usually spend so much energy on their
caring tasks that they have none left over for themselves.
Constantly drained, tired and powerless to change their
situation, it is not surprising that their mental health
suffers.

Another frequent result is the deterioration of other relationships. We have already seen how carers can become
isolated because their friends and other members of their
families stop keeping in contact, and the strain that caring
can place on other relationships.

One of the most serious effects caring can have, however, is on marriages. Sometimes it may result in drawing
couples together:

*My husband has been a great support to me while I've been looking
after Mum. He is still at work, even though he has mild MS. At
weekends he will sit with her while I shop or have a day with my
daughter at Warwick. Never once has he said for her to go into a
home and his understanding attitude has helped him and me to talk
about things more than we've ever done in our 30 years together.*

All too frequently, however, the strain is very great:

I don't live with my father but I go to see him every day, and I feel

*torn between him and my husband all the time. It's got a lot worse
since Ronnie, my husband, has been retired, as before he never
needed to know how often I saw Dad. Now, whenever I'm with
Dad I'm worried about what Ronnie will think, and if I say to Dad
I'm going home I feel guilty leaving him on his own for the rest of
the day. Sometimes on a Sunday we all go out and have our dinner
in a pub, but only if Ronnie is in the mood for Dad, which isn't
often. At holiday times Ronnie and I argue because I have to go and
see Dad when we could be going out together. I dread the day when
Dad gets worse and has to come to live with us, as it would be hell
on earth.*

*My wife suffers from rheumatoid arthritis and for sixteen years
has been getting steadily worse. Not one person has ever asked me
how I've coped for sixteen years. I used to have a large allotment
and keep racing pigeons and go to the pub for a couple of pints, but
I've had to pack it all in to care for my wife. Sometimes, when my
wife is crying with pain, I feel I can't stand it any more and I get
my coat on and feel I'll leave, but I only walk to the corner shop to
get a packet of fags and then I go back and start again. I feel so
guilty, but sometimes I hate her and long to divorce her.*

Divorce is of course a very common occurrence. We have
no statistics about this, but judging by my letters, the rate
must be high among carers:

*My marriage finished a bit back as old people can be very demand-
ing and some people haven't much of a caring or patient outlook.
My husband had an affair with another woman and I know it's
really my fault because our married life was affected. I was always
tired or worried that Mum would call out in the middle of it all.*

*During my marriage I found the strain intolerable, with both
my husband and my mother seemingly fighting for dominance
over me, and because of her disability my mother had to come first.
It's not just the physical caring which causes the strain, but the fact
that you are trying to accommodate another person with a mind
and will-power of her own. Any normal marriage just can't stand
that.*

Divorce sometimes means that the strain of caring falls on another family member — perhaps even on a child. The most common situation on the files of Carers National Association is where a formerly happy home falls apart when the wife develops multiple sclerosis in her late twenties or early thirties and the husband, unable to cope, leaves. The children take up the burden.

One remarkable fact is that the breakdown of a marriage while caring does not always mean that the caring itself stops. We quite frequently receive letters from spouses who are divorced but still cannot be free of the caring role. This letter is a typical case:

Our marriage was never really a wild success. He was twelve years older and our interests didn't really coincide. We stayed together for the children, but I was determined to go when they left home. When my son was about to go to university I met this man — he was nice and kind. I suppose I'd say I fell in love with him if it doesn't sound too soft. Well, anyway, just as we were making arrangements to go off to Wales together, my husband was diagnosed with Motor Neurone disease. The divorce was already underway and we went ahead with it, but I never left — how could I? The other man said he'd wait for me, but that was eight years ago and of course he grew tired of waiting. Well, he waited two years, you could not expect more than that, could you?

BEREAVEMENT

One of the most difficult emotional strains of all for carers happens when the caring stops, when the person they are caring for dies.

We have to remember that this final bereavement is the culmination of what can be seen as a series of bereavements for the carer. She has suffered the loss of her own life, her own status; she has suffered the loss of other relationships, possibly also the 'loss' of the person for whom she has been caring because of the sort of personality change which can happen with some illnesses or disabilities. She may also have had to cope with the loss one feels when the person for whom one is caring finally has to enter some kind of residential care. Now she suffers the bereavement resulting from the death of the person cared for, and with that loss comes an equally great one — the loss of the caring role which she had grown so used to.

My mother always believed I'd do everything for her and I resented that so much, but now she's gone I think I'm on the verge of a nervous breakdown. If I had the choice I would have her back and go through it all again. I have so much time on my hands now, I don't know what to do with myself. I have the chance to go out and do anything I want, but I don't want to bother. I miss my Mum more than anyone knows and as I write this, the tears are dripping on the paper.

I just can't seem to adjust to the fact that I won't hear him banging on the ceiling with his stick any more. When I think how it used to wind me up, and now I'd give anything in the world to hear it again.

People think I'm going mad because I talk about Estelle all the time. Other people lose children and have to come to terms with it. But they don't realise what it's like to lose something that's been your LIFE for eight years.

However bad it is, you never stop hoping for a miracle — maybe they'll find a cure for Alzheimer's Disease tomorrow and my husband will be as he used to be. It's a bitter blow when you have to come to terms with there being no miracle — or if there is one, it'll be too late for him.

The familiar feelings of guilt return at the time of death, even if they'd ever gone away.

I don't know how other people have felt, but I do know that after my husband and Dad died I felt guilty because I felt in a way relieved that I could go to bed at night and sleep.

Every time I was impatient with him, every time I kept him waiting, every time I didn't love him as I should, comes back to haunt me now he's gone. I had prayed for his death many times when I saw him in pain, but now those prayers come back to haunt me even though he's at peace.

The carer may also be tortured by thoughts of whether the decisions taken in the course of caring were the right ones. These may be about letting the person go into residential care — 'Was I right to send him in there, even though he was so well looked after?' — but also about whether it was right to take on the caring role at all.

I thought I did the right thing, taking my parents to live with us, but now I wonder if I wouldn't have been better to leave them to cope alone and therefore force the services to help them. This is not only because of the strain on me and my family, though nothing prepared me for the strain of coping with a senile person or watching the deterioration of someone so loved. No, I'm thinking of the effect my intervention had on their relationship — it took the power away from them somehow, and must have stopped them having any chance of communicating together as they used to.

If I had said I wouldn't take it on, would he be alive today?

Could a hospital have kept a child like her alive longer than I did?

Was I cruel to look after him so well, he lived three years longer than anyone expected him to?

Many of these feelings are familiar in any bereavement situation. For carers, however, they are much more acute: the readjustment problems are greater because the caring role has been so all-consuming. Their problems may be even further compounded because they are often denied even the dignity of mourning. It is extraordinary how often carers report being told, 'I expect it's a happy release,' when a much loved dependant dies. People do not mean to be heartless, but 'happy release' is just about the last thing the carer wants to hear at a time when a life without caring seems almost impossible to contemplate.

The turmoil of emotions to which carers have been subject in their caring years, and the strain of coping with them, do not equip them well for making a swift adjustment to a different kind of life-style, even though they may have been wishing for it throughout the caring period.

4 Background and History

Caring has not just been invented. Most of us have an image in our minds of sick elderly or frail people being cared for within the bosom of their families, and of the people who were doing the caring often showing extremes of selflessness, devotion and commitment. We may have gleaned these images from literature. Think, for example, of Jane Austen's heroine Emma Woodhouse, whose concern for the health of her father prevents her initially from accepting her suitor's offer of marriage. Or the selfless behaviour of Miss Sedley in *Vanity Fair*, giving up her life to care for her odious father. We may also draw conclusions about caring from real characters in history, such as Elizabeth Barrett Browning and Florence Nightingale. Knowledge we have gained from other generations, and attitudes about it being 'better in the old days' or 'people looked after their own in the old days,' further influence the way we feel.

This received wisdom is in fact fairly inaccurate. *Exactly the same proportion of elderly and handicapped people are in residential care now as at the beginning of the twentieth century.* About five per cent only are cared for in residential settings. The rest live either alone or with their families. Consider too the accuracy of the picture we have in our minds of selfless devotion to spouses who were chronically ill. *The average length of a marriage in the mid-nineteenth century was twelve years.* Death did then what divorce does now. True, there were no antibiotics or kidney machines, but it is a mistake to assume that the caring period was necessarily prolonged. To put it bluntly, people died more quickly!

At the beginning of this century a man had a life expectancy of 48 years and a woman 52 years. By the beginning of the 1980s, a male could be expected to live until 70 and a female until 78 years.

People in the United Kingdom are living longer, not only into old age but also surviving longer with handicaps and certain forms of illness. This would not necessarily have led to carers coming into focus more sharply, had it not been accompanied by a change in government policy.

It has been the development of so-called 'Care in the Community' policies which have led to interest in carers. The idea that it is better to care for people in the community rather than in some form of institution is not a new one: it probably dates from the days of the workhouse, which was the last refuge of those no longer able to care for themselves. There was enormous shame attached to 'going into an institution', when the institutions concerned were either the workhouse, thus proving you had no money and no family to care for you, or the asylum, thus proving you were not sane enough to care for yourself. This shame appears to be deeply embedded in our national consciousness and has influenced the development of social policies in this century.

There is no simple definition of what 'Community Care' means. The word 'Community' itself defies definition. There is a famous article, much quoted in the 'sixties, which describes finding no fewer than 94 definitions of the word! The only common theme was that they all dealt with people. As the word has come to be used in relation to social policies, however, it is taken to mean care which is provided outside an institution. Largely, then, it means care in the receiver's home.

In 1972 Kathleen Jones gave the following definition of Community Care:

To the politician community care is a useful piece of rhetoric, to the sociologist it is a stick to beat institutional care with, to the civil servant it is a cheap alternative to institutional care which can be passed to the local authorities for action, or inaction. To the visionary it is a dream of a new society in which people really do care; to social services departments it is a nightmare of heightened public expectations and inadequate resources to meet them. We are only just beginning to find out what it means to the old, the chronic sick and the handicapped.

There was at this time no reference to carers — in fact there was little reference to how this community care would be provided at all. In those days community care was largely about closing hospital beds. To see how ideas about community care have developed, we need to look at the needs of the four priority groups — that is, people who are mentally ill, mentally handicapped, physically handicapped or elderly.

Mentally Ill

The idea that mentally ill people were better cared for in the community rather than in large institutions was quite common as long ago as the 1930s. The development of the idea stood still during the Second World War and began to regain momentum during the 1950s. The peak of hospital bed occupancy was in 1954 and has been declining steadily ever since. It was accelerated in the early 1960s by a series of scandals about the conditions in which mentally ill patients were being treated. The public outrage at the Ely and other enquiries had several effects — one can, for example, date the encouragement of volunteers to go into long stay institutions like Ely to these scandals. It was felt that if ordinary members of the public were able to frequent these places, which previously had often had a policy of positively discouraging even the visits of relatives, then the same kind of conditions which had caused such distress could not possibly arise again.

The first appointment of Voluntary Service Co-ordinators was made in the late 1960s, and most Health Authorities pursued an active policy of encouraging members of the public to become involved in a more active way than the previous work with volunteers, which had largely been confined to providing tea bars and trolley services.

In 1975 the then Labour government published a White Paper, *Better Services for the Mentally Ill*, in which the Secretary of State, Mrs Barbara Castle, proposed a new model of care and set out four policy objectives:

1   The expansion of Local Authority personal social services to provide residential, domiciliary, day care and social work support.
2   The relocation of specialist services in local settings.
3   The establishment of the right organisational links.
4   A significant improvement in staffing.

The report set out details of how the services should operate. For example, the specialist services should be based at a psychiatric hospital which would act as a hub for the services and provide the in-patient treatment. In-patient stays were reducing and it was therefore to be expected that the services provided by this hospital (which was likely in the future to be the District General Hospital rather than a specialist psychiatric hospital), would radiate outwards from the hospital to a range of clinics, health centres, and the patient's own home. Special mention was made of the increasing number of elderly mentally frail people, and it was recommended that each health district should have an assessment unit within it, with both day care and long-term facilities for the elderly mentally ill. The White Paper also emphasised that, in addition to the Health Service provisions, there should be developed a range of social services provisions.

Various forms of residential accommodations are needed to cater for different degrees of dependency and for different lengths of stay. Day centres need a variety of facilities which, within a single establishment, can be used flexibly to give effective help to each individual. Residential and day care services should be conceived not as a self-contained system but as part of a broad range of options extending beyond the health and personal social services — for helping the mentally ill.

In addition to these recommendations about the mentally ill, the White Paper also mentioned the need to provide services for people with special needs, such as those who slept out, alcoholics and drugs addicts.

Mentally Handicapped

In 1971, a White Paper, *Better Services for the Mentally Handicapped*, outlined the principles by which a policy of Community Care for the mentally handicapped should operate. It stressed that within 20 years there should be a total shift from services based in hospital to services based in the community. This required considerable expansion in social services, since the National Health Service Act of 1959 had given Local Authorities the duty of providing community services for the mentally handicapped, including residential accommodation and day care.

Within three years it became apparent that progress towards Community Care was not taking place as fast as might have been hoped, and in 1975 Mrs Barbara Castle announced three new initiatives:

1   The National Development Group for mentally handicapped people would be set up.
2   A Committee of Enquiry into mental handicap nursing and care would be established.
3   A Development Team would be set up to offer advice and assistance to health services and Local Authorities in the planning and delivery of services to mentally handicapped people.

PHYSICALLY HANDICAPPED

With the two groups above, government guidelines lay down the amount of provisions which must be made, but in the case of this group and the one following, this is not so. Rather a framework of principles has been established, within which care in the community has been expected to develop. In 1970, the Chronically Sick and Disabled Persons Act strengthened the commitment to Community Care in various ways. For example:

1 It required Local Authorities to identify younger disabled people in their areas and to make known its services.
2 It placed a duty on Local Authorities to provide practical assistance, recreational and educational facilities, help with transport, adaptations to the home, help with holidays, meals and telephones.
3 It required the provision of access and sanitary facilities for disabled people in public buildings.
4 It promoted representation on advisory committees concerned with disability.
5 It introduced the yellow badge system for parking and access.

In addition, the handbook for the health and personal social services, *Care in Action*, published in 1981, set out the following objectives:

— Relieve pressure on caring relatives through more short term care and treatment (including day care), development of services for the incontinent, of care attendant schemes and, perhaps through the development of voluntary bodies and community groups, of other supporting services for disabled people and their families.

— Further improve arrangements for caring for younger disabled people separately from elderly people.

— Help those with hearing impairments to make the best of an improved range of aids, in particular the recruitment and training of additional hearing therapists.

— Improve co-operation between authorities to ensure that visually handicapped people, particularly elderly people, are aware of and can benefit from the services and advice which should be available to them. Services for newly blind people should be improved. They should be able to receive teaching in daily living skills and support necessary to achieve independence in the community.

ELDERLY

The case for community care for the elderly was very much strengthened by the publication in 1967 of *Sans Everything* (Robb). It contained evidence from patients and nurses of appalling ill-treatment of older people in geriatric and psycho-geriatric wards. It indicated that many older people in these institutions were stripped of clothes and all their personal possessions, subjected to ill-treatment and to loss of individuality.

Guidance as to how care for the elderly should change from residential based to community based is the least specific of all. *Care in Action* set out objectives, though in very vague terms:

1   Strengthen the primary and Community Care services, together with neighbourhood and voluntary support, to enable elderly people to live at home.
2   Encourage an active approach to treatment and rehabilitation, to enable elderly people to return to the Community from hospital whenever possible.
3   Maintain an adequate provision for the minority of elderly people requiring long term care in hospital or residential homes.

The White Paper of 1981, *Growing Older*, gave an indication that the contribution of family and friends to the care of older people was recognised.

Whatever level of expenditure proves practicable and however it is distributed, the primary sources of support and care for elderly people are informal and voluntary. These spring from the personal ties of kinship, friendship and neighbourhood. They are irreplaceable.

It is the role of public authorities to sustain and, where necessary, develop — but never to displace — such support and care.

For all four of these groups there were strong humanitarian grounds for developing care in the community policies, but no one could deny that there were economic grounds also. Because care in hospital or residential home has always been expensive and has grown increasingly so in recent years, an idea grew up that Community Care was a cheaper option. This is because calculations about the cost of Community Care have always tended to ignore the 'costs', which are thus transferred to family, friends, neighbours and voluntary organisations. Calculations also rarely take account of the facts that Community Care is not provided 24-hourly (except by carers), unlike the care in an institution. Good — that is, comprehensive — Community Care is not in fact likely to be cheaper, but its development has undoubtedly been accelerated by the misguided notion that it *is*.

By 1986 there was general agreement that Community Care was the 'best thing', *but* a growing disquiet with how it was being delivered. Unsatisfactory social security arrangements had funded a boom in private and voluntary residential care, while care at home was under-resourced. The state would pay the *full* cost of residential care for anyone on supplementary benefit, for example, while only paying £24.00 per week to a carer, and nothing at all to a carer over retiring age. This culminated in the publication in 1986 of the Audit Commission's report, focusing on the shambles which many believed Community Care had become. Called *Making a Reality of Community Care*, the review pointed out that funding arrangements, responsibility, staffing and joint planning between health services and Local Authorities were in some disarray and that the result was poor value for money. It called for a radical review of the services. The government's response was to appoint Sir Roy Griffiths to undertake a review. He spent 15 months reviewing the way Community Care was operating, and in March 1988 produced *Community Care — An Agenda for Action*.

THE GRIFFITHS REVIEW

In his review Sir Roy Griffiths said, 'If community care means anything it is that responsibility is placed as near to the individual and his carers as possible.' He proposed that central government should take Community Care more seriously by designating a Minister to provide policy leadership and direction, and that Local Authorities should take the lead role within policy guidelines specified by the appropriate Minister and in collaboration with relevant agencies. Named individuals would be given the budget and responsibility for delivering care to clearly identified recipients who would enjoy more consumer choice. The Local Authorities should become purchasers and organisers of care, rather than simply be direct providers.

Sir Roy did not press for extra resources because it was not in his brief, although he certainly implied that more resources were required.

I have insisted that we should be open as to what we are seeking to achieve and be realistic as to what policies can be pursued with the likely money available. What cannot be acceptable is to allow ambitious policies to be embarked on without adequate funds. On many counts poorly implemented programmes for change are very often worse than the status quo.

In general the Griffiths Review was received favourably by Local Authorities and by the voluntary sector. Health Authorities were more guarded in their welcome for the proposals but even so the majority of managers were in favour and firmly of the opinion that change was necessary. Government reactions, however, were very slow in coming and at the time of going to press (December 1988) no official reaction had been published, although there was known to be much work in progress at the Department of Health. The decision, in July 1988, to split the Department of Health and Social Security into two separate ministries no doubt added to the delay. All those who are concerned with the delivery of Community Care have accepted that, as the report says, 'Doing nothing is not an option' and await the Government reactions with impatience.

More than any previous report, the Griffiths Review emphasised the contribution of carers and the fact that it did so was largely due to the growth by 1986 of the 'carers movement'.

WHAT ABOUT THE CARERS?

In 1965 the National Council for the Single Woman and her Dependants was founded by the Rev. Mary Webster. Having in effect sacrificed her career to look after her parents, she had become aware of the effect this had had upon her and realised that there were many other single women in similar circumstances. At that time, if parents needed care, it was likely to be the unmarried daughter with a career who was expected to give up work to do the caring, since careers for women were not then considered to be of any great importance. Mary Webster was an exceptional woman and set about trying to alleviate for the carers the loneliness and isolation she had herself experienced. She felt that the isolation could be eased by forming an organisation with local branches, where carers could meet regularly for mutual support. But she saw campaigning work as being of equal importance, and from the beginning NCSWD acted as a forceful pressure group. Many of its members, like Mary Webster, were professional women, articulate and well educated, who had felt confined, frustrated and oppressed in their caring role. They now found an outlet for their considerable energies and threw themselves into campaigning.

Throughout its first ten years the organisation grew steadily. It campaigned for and achieved an income for those who had to give up work to care — the Invalid Care Allowance. In addition, the constant Attendance Allowance was granted to those being cared for, and the Dependent Relative's Tax Allowance was brought in.

NCSWD was active in providing housing either directly, through Housing Associations, or indirectly, by protecting housing rights for former carers who might be threatened with eviction.

It undertook to educate the public through the media and through publishing a series of reports describing the circumstances and needs of its members. At the same time, branches were established in local areas, to provide mutual support and social activities for carers.

Although the organisation was very successful in this work, the impression one has today is that what it brought sharply into focus in the public mind was not carers, but single women, with the emphasis on their caring role as something of a secondary issue.

By the end of the '70s there was increasing recognition that circumstances were changing and that the organisation must change, too. Single women were decreasing in number, and the responsibility of looking after elderly parents was now falling more upon married couples. Also, at a time of lengthening life expectancy, more frail and elderly dependants were being cared for by spouses rather than daughters. Accordingly, in 1982 the organisation decided to change its name and its constituency, and to extend its membership to all those who had the care of an elderly dependant. It became the National Council for Carers and their Elderly Dependants.

In 1981 Judith Oliver began the process of forming an organisation which would address itself to the needs and wants of all family caregivers. The anger which she had felt as a result of being unable to get help, at a period when she herself needed medical treatment, was converted into positive action.

A new organisation was necessary, since there was nothing for carers involved in a situation where those they were caring for were not elderly. We know that there are common needs among carers, whatever the age or disability of those they care for, and it was necessary to draw attention to the position of younger wives and husbands, and of parents of handicapped young adults (and children), as well as to the needs of carers of the elderly, who are statistically in the majority.

From the beginning, The Association of Carers' philosophy was that the differences among carers stemmed from their own personal position: labelling them by the disability or age of the person they were caring for could diminish the attention paid to their own personal needs. It launched itself with a 'high profile' in the media, and this increased with the campaign to get Invalid Care Allowance for married women. Originally granted in 1976 to single women and male carers, benefit was not available to married women until 1986, when a married woman, Mrs Jacqueline Drake, was awarded Invalid Care Allowance for the first time.

The case gained huge publicity for carers, because it was taken to the European Parliament and the Advocate General decided that the British Government was in breach of the EEC Directive on Equal Treatment in denying Invalid Care Allowance to married and co-habiting women. The European Court of Justice was due to ratify the Advocate General's decision on 24th June: on 23rd June the British Government announced that it would extend the Invalid Care Allowance to married women. A case, as one newspaper commented, of 'being hanged in the morning concentrates the mind wonderfully'!

A CARERS' DEBATE

On 1st May 1986, a debate on carers was held in the House of Commons. The opposition moved an amendment calling for adequate respite care, a flexible system of support services, and for the extension of the Invalid Care Allowance to married women. Summing up the debate, the then Minister for Social Security, Tony Newton, said:

> The one thing on which all hon. Members are united is the importance of the subject that we have been debating for over two hours. In some ways, the time has been too short for such an importance subject. In the past, the people about whom we have been talking have had inadequate recognition, perhaps from hon. Members on both sides of the House. Such people are worthy not only of the admiration that has been expressed by every hon. Member who has spoken, but of the support of the whole community for what they do.
>
> Apart from the occasional rude remarks that have been made about the Government, and the odd sour note that has crept in, I found the debate immensely encouraging.
>
> I suspect that five, or certainly ten years ago, such a debate would not have taken place, because nobody would have thought the subject warranted even two or three hours of the time of the House. That is a sign of great and welcome increase in public and political awareness of the problems of carers.

The amendment was defeated by 272 votes to 170, but at the end of the debate it was resolved to add the following words:

> That this House, noting that there are a substantial number of people from the age of seven to 70 years caring for disabled and elderly relatives at home, often for many years, pays the warmest possible tribute to these carers; and further noting the research which shows that carers themselves often suffer from mental and physical illness, social isolation and disadvantage, recognises the action already taken by the Government to improve their position, especially in view of

the undoubted savings to public funds which flow from their commitment; and in particular welcomes the Government's intentions, in line with its stated policies on care in the community and the availability of resources, that (a) adequate respite care, both at home and in short-stay facilities, be assured by continuing improvement in the level of support given to statutory and voluntary agencies, (b) a flexible system of appropriate support such as home helps and home nursing be available at times when the carer needs them and (c) any judgement which may be made by the European Court relating to the invalid care allowance introduced by the Labour Government in 1976, be carefully considered by the Government and made the subject of a report to the House.

HELPING THE COMMUNITY TO CARE

In June 1984, under increasing pressure about Community Care, the Government had announced its 'Helping the Community to Care' initiatives, which were aimed at helping carers. There were two main elements:

1   Demonstration Districts

The DHSS funded a consortium of voluntary organisations in each of three districts (East Sussex, Stockport and Sandwell), to make grants to local voluntary organisations to initiate, extend and improve the services they provide of relevance to informal carers. Funding was in the order of £200,000 a year for each of three years in each district.

The Demonstration Districts were intended to enhance general understanding of the best ways of supporting carers in the community, and to examine the implications of this kind of delegated funding. The project provided an opportunity to evaluate this kind of 'demonstration' as a way of developing and testing innovative responses to particular problems.

Monitoring and evaluation of the projects was undertaken by the Tavistock Institute, and all three districts engaged with the research team in a process of self-evaluation of funded schemes and in the exploration of wider issues. The main objectives of the evaluation and monitoring were:

— to monitor and identify outcomes and indicators for the future
— to provide data for use in other areas.

Much valuable work was done by the Demonstration Districts and there is no doubt that support for carers will have been greatly increased as a result, not only in the Districts themselves but also in other areas too. The increased support for carers sometimes took the form of enhanced support for existing voluntary organisations, at others it consisted of developing completely new services. But one of the most important aspects of the work of the Districts was the way in which they promoted change in a wider sense, by raising awareness and providing information about carers and their needs to statutory and voluntary services.

2   *Information for Carers*

To improve the availability and range of information to individual carers, self-help groups and professionals in their work with carers, an 'Informal Care Support Unit' was set up at the King's Fund Centre. It aimed to strengthen support for carers, develop and produce information for carers and professionals, and to identify areas where more work was needed.

DISABLED PERSONS ACT 1986

In July 1986 carers appeared in legislation for the first time. This was in the entitled Disabled Persons (Services, Consultation and Representation) Act 1986.

Because of the massive resources likely to be required to

provide better services for disabled people, the Act is to be implemented in stages. However, several parts relating to carers were implemented that year. Section 4 of the Act confirms that a Local Authority must assess the need of a disabled person for services if asked by the person *or* the carer. Section 2 requires Social Services Departments to make arrangements for the provision of a variety of services if they are satisfied that they are needed by anyone who is permanently and substantially handicapped. These services include help in the home, aids and adaptations, recreational facilities in the home, holidays, meals and telephones. Section 8 is the most important for carers. It concerns people (other than paid staff) who are providing 'a substantial amount of care' for a disabled person living at home. It requires a Local Authority *to have regard to their ability to continue to provide care on a regular basis*, when they are assessing the need of a disabled person for any of the social services.

Although few Local Authorities are as yet acting on these new regulations, their becoming law was an extremely important milestone for carers. There had been pressure from carers groups to have the wording of the Act made stronger, but the advice of those negotiating its passage through Parliament was that this might result in a dilution of its effect for disabled people. Pushing the interests of carers was seen as counter-productive to the needs of the disabled. This was disappointing, but there was some consolation in the fact that carers' needs were acknowledged in the Act and that the occupation of caring was at last enshrined in legislation.

5   The Professionals

In Chapter 2 we looked at the people who help carers, who give them access to services, who give them advice and counselling treatment — in short, those people who act as *gatekeepers* to the services which are so essential to carers. These people are collectively referred to as 'professionals'. This chapter looks at the relationship between carers and professionals.

The first thing to say about this relationship is that for the great majority there is *no relationship at all*.

In 1986, when the then opposition spokesperson on the Health and Social Services conducted a survey in conjunction with the Association of Carers, he found that 83 per cent of them received *no help whatsoever* with their caring from anyone at all. That is to say, not from another family member, from any neighbour and from no professional of any kind. The OPCS survey of 1988 found that of 1.7 million carers who live in the same household as the person cared for, 66 per cent receive no help at all.

For those who do have some kind of contact with professionals, I should say at the outset that many have good experiences and satisfactory, helpful relationships.

The help given to us was excellent, the nurses were kind and caring, and we only had to ask and they tried to arrange help for us. A bath lady came once a week, incontinence pads were delivered regularly and the doctor came any time I called.

I really feel my social worker cares about ME, not just about Sally. She comes to see if I need help, not just to see a mentally handicapped child on her patch.

Sadly, though, for every carer who says, 'The doctor in the hospital made us apply for the attendance allowance and it's been a godsend,' there are others who say, 'I only found out about the allowances after five years — why didn't anyone tell me?' For every carer who says, 'At no time did I feel pressured into keeping my husband at home, I felt all of them, social worker, doctor and nurses, were trying to help us make a decision which would be right for everyone,' we are in contact with others who say, 'I told the doctor and the social worker I couldn't cope, or rather that I didn't think I'd be able to, and they just said, "We are discharging her tomorrow and that's it." And discharge her they did.'

The following account from a woman living in the north of England is fairly typical of the cases recounted daily to Carers National Association.

When my grandmother went senile, I was determined to look after her. I am her only relative so there was no one else to share the work. At first I tried to look after her in her own home, but that proved impossible as she couldn't be left alone for any length of time, and as I had a husband and son I could not actually move in with her. I found the DHSS very helpful at this time. When I explained that Gran was buying ridiculous things with her pension and not buying food or paying rent, etc., they came to talk to her and then made me the appointed payee for her pension and supplementary benefit, and also told me how to apply for clothing allowance, bathing allowance, etc. In fact, of all the people I had to deal with, I found the DHSS the most sympathetic and helpful. We gave Gran's flat up and moved her in with us. As we had only two bedrooms we made a makeshift partition in my son's room, and gave Gran and my son half each. This proved far from ideal, as Gran's day and night were reversed, and she would spend the time when the household was trying to sleep singing and tapping on the walls.

I then approached social services to see if any help would be available to build her her own separate bedroom. The social worker's answer to this was to tell me to put Gran in a home. In fact, the social worker came three times with offers of places in homes for Gran, despite my having said that I had no intention of putting her in a home. I found the social worker's attitude most unhelpful and at times even antagonistic. She told us that grant aid by social services had been cut by the government, so there was no possibility of having the house adapted to accommodate Gran. I accepted this and three months passed.

Then Nana had a thrombosis and had to have first her foot, then her leg amputated. When she came home from hospital, we found it desperately hard to look after her. My husband and I had to carry her upstairs and downstairs each day. This was a strain as my husband was waiting to go into hospital for an operation and really shouldn't have been lifting. We also couldn't get the wheelchair through the kitchen doorway into the toilet, and that made another carrying job. I approached the Citizens' Advice Bureau who advised me to write to my MP. He was most helpful: someone from social services came round and we filled in all the forms for a chairlift on the stairs and for a downstairs bedroom to be built — also for a bath hoist to make getting Nana in and out of the bath a little easier.

I expected all this to take a couple of months before work started. However, it was a year before work was started on the bedroom, and still there was no sign of the bath hoist or chairlift. I became desperate as my husband had had his operation and I was having to carry Nana up to the bathroom each day as she was doubly incontinent, and also to the toilet. I wrote to my MP again, and my doctor and district nurse made urgent phone calls (I had finally managed to convince them how bad it was) to social services to say that, though the downstairs bedroom was marvellous, we desperately needed the chairlift, bath hoist and kitchen doorway widening. Nothing happened, so I wrote to my MP again. In the meantime Nana's remaining foot turned gangrenous, and she was taken into hospital and died two days later, after an operation.

I have told you all this because, though I know that it would never have been an easy task to look after Nana, it was made far harder by not getting the adaptations and by what seemed to be the complete lack of communication between bits of the Council. I was also mentally strained by having to fight for these things, and I am sure a lot of people would not have had the energy or inclination to do so.

I must say I found social services useless. I felt as though I was a lot of trouble to the social worker and was told several times to put Gran in a home if it was such a struggle managing without the adaptations. The district nurse just offered platitudes and did very little to help. In fact I rarely saw her. When I asked for bath nurses for Gran, I was told that they were understaffed and overworked. I begged to be put on the laundry list and was told I needed to be desperate before she could get this for me. Since I WAS desperate I called her out on the pretext of seeing Gran, who was not well, and showed her the blankets, sheets and pillow cases that Nana had soiled the night before and explained that this happened every night. The district nurse said she could see what it was like and sympathised, but she could only put so many homes on the laundry list at any one time, so I would need to wait till someone died. I then wrote to my MP and told a lie, saying I had no washer, and I got put on the laundry service that same week. Likewise, when Nana was getting worse, I asked to have the one day that she went to the day centre increased. Yet again I was told there was a waiting list. In the end I paid for her to attend a private home two days a week. This was expensive and I had to pay for it out of Gran's attendance allowance since we were on supplementary benefit as my husband was unemployed.

To conclude, I must say that the help for the elderly in this area was nonexistent, and at times I felt that because of Gran's age everyone thought she was worthless and that neither she nor I was worth the bother.

The carer in this account was visited by at least seven different professionals, yet none of them was able to alleviate her problems until she put up a fight.

It is, of course, extremely difficult for carers to know just who the professionals are. How on earth are they expected to know what is the difference between a physiotherapist and an occupational therapist? Still less to distinguish the plethora of initials by which these people are known to their colleagues. The initials MSW, CPN, DGH (Medical Social Worker, Community Psychiatric Nurse, District General Hospital) mean something if you are working with them; they are simply a mystery to anyone else.

Well, I don't rightly know who this lady was who came to see us about getting help — from the Council, was she? Or perhaps the doctor sent her? Anyway, I think she came about getting a rail put in the bathroom for Dad to hang onto. But that was a year ago. I did ring up about it a few months on but no one seemed to know what was the right department to speak to and I couldn't hang on any longer because Dad was needing the toilet.

Professions develop and progress. Those working in the field know, for example, that an occupational therapist is concerned with helping people to adjust to their environment and to manage better in their own homes, but to the carer an OT may be associated in her mind with some vague and long-held memory of a lady doing basketry and knitting to help bored patients in hospital. An approach to an OT for that kind of help might not be very happily received. Similarly, a request to a social worker for help which is more properly provided by a home help may create difficult relationships, as it may offend the social worker's sensibilities about how she is perceived by the carer.

These professionals are gatekeepers to services and to information, yet many carers remain totally in ignorance of what may be available. What are some of the reasons for this?

First, there are the practicalities. Carers may simply never be in contact with any professionals at all. As I said in Chapter 1, many carers never recognise themselves as carers. It never even enters their heads that there is anyone at all out there who can help them, still less that they have any rights to this help.

I mean, it just didn't occur to me to ask for help — well you don't, do you? You just know it's your duty and you should get on with it. Mind, I've thought many a time since that someone ought to have offered and made damned sure I accepted.

Second, it may be that there is absolutely no help available to that particular carer. This would be a rare situation. Although the help which the carer feels she wants may not be available, there are certainly likely to be some services in her area. A Local Authority may be able to offer two days a week day care, for example, whereas what the carer feels she needs is someone to come into the home and relieve her five mornings a week.

Third, it may be that the carer is so shocked by the impact of a crisis that she is unable to take in the information about the professionals who are there to help her when it is given to her. The crisis may be sudden, at the point of discharge from a hospital, for example; or the situation may have been going on for such a long time that the carer is near breaking point and unable to take in anything which is said to her. This may result in services being offered which the carer turns down, either because she is too shocked to accept or because she does not appreciate that she will need them.

They did offer me a laundry service, I think, when George first had his stroke, but quite honestly, I didn't think then that I'd need it. And after he got worse I didn't know where to go for it because I couldn't remember who I'd been speaking to. In any case, I suppose once you've turned something down that's it.

These things certainly do prevent carers receiving the help they so badly need, but in my experience, what much more frequently gets in the way of good communication between carers and professionals is the attitude which each group has towards the other.

How do Professionals feel about Carers?

My impression is that, until very recently, they did not feel anything about them at all. When was the first research done about carers? When was the first training course about carers put on? Very recently — probably only within the last five years. True, the problem has grown larger in recent years because of the increase in the elderly population, together with Care in the Community policies; but caring, and the problems which are faced by carers, have always been with us. In 1976, when Pat Gay and I were researching our book about the problems faced by patients when they were discharged from hospital, we found many people suffering greatly from lack of planning, co-ordination and co-operation, but our focus was very much on what happened to the patient. We produced a book, *When I Went Home*, from our research, and when I reread it recently, I was very struck by the fact that, although we found many problems among the families of the discharged patients, we paid them almost no attention. We often mentioned the people we would now call carers without really drawing any conclusions about the distress they were in.

> Sometimes a relative would accompany us back to the car after our interview with the discharged patient, and would express their fears:
> 'I need a break so badly — how can I get one?'
> 'I've been looking after her now for nine long years.'
> 'However will I manage if he gets worse?'

None of the recommendations we made or the solutions we suggested concerned the carers, however. All our attention was focused on the sick person, as was everyone's in those days.

Among some professionals, this situation still exists. Not long ago I was at a meeting with many eminent members of the medical profession. We were discussing the problems which surfaced when an elderly person was discharged from hospital. The distinguished consultant who chaired my small group opened our discussion by saying, 'Of course we must realise that when an elderly person is discharged from hospital the whole burden of care falls on the general practitioner.' Every other member of the group (mostly other distinguished medical people) nodded sagely in agreement. I requested further clarification of this point, asking, for example, how often the GP visited, how long the visits lasted and so on. I was told that the GP had to visit sometimes as often as twice a week and the visits could last as long as twenty minutes! With some difficulty I kept quiet and waited to see how long it would take them to realise what they were really saying. It took 25 minutes for one of them to turn to me and say, 'Oh, I see what you mean, the carer is there all the time.'

In my experience, ignoring the carer in this way is not malicious. It is simply that none of their training has ever taught them to recognise the carer. On the contrary, it has all been focused on the dependent person, the patient, the person being cared for. And as we have already seen, there may well be an essential conflict between the needs of the person cared for and the carer.

In my work I usually find that there are three common attitudes which many professionals hold towards carers. They may ignore them, they may feel guilty about them or they may be impatient with them.

They may Ignore Them

We have already looked at one aspect of this — at actually not seeing carers because nothing in your experience has helped you to do so. The other aspect is when professionals ignore the carer because they know, or rather fear, that they will be unable to help. They are afraid even to enter into a dialogue at all. The fear will so often stem from a knowledge of lack of resources, an awareness that if the carer's needs are actually identified, the professional will be totally unable to meet them anyway and will be left feeling inadequate and guilty.

'What the hell will I do if they say they can't do the caring, when I know damned well that there are no beds in the hospital, no places in day care and that the family can't afford private care?' said a GP. Sometimes the carer will be asked a certain set of questions to which the professional knows he has the answers, for example, 'Can we get you a hand rail fixed?' or 'Do you need someone to help you bath him once a week?' But they are not asked the questions which actually might be more important, such as, 'How do you feel about your husband?' 'How well do you and your mother get on?'

'I don't ask those questions because I'm afraid to hear the answers,' said the doctor. This may be entirely understandable — professionals are after all human — but it can lead to extreme situations such as the one I have encountered several times.

The first time I had this experience with a carer, I was slow to pick up what the problem was. The carer sounded quite calm as she described to me the arrangements which were being made to discharge her father to her after he had been in hospital. The doctor and the nurses with whom she was in contact were making the assumption which is usually made, that is, there is a daughter, and in this case a daughter who was at home and seemingly free to do the caring, therefore the old man would be discharged to her. I made an assumption too, that this situation was like many others I hear about every day — the carer was worried about how she would cope and was needing from me some kind of guidance about the level of support she could expect. As our conversation went on, however, I found that this particular carer was in fact being offered a very high level of support, and a great deal of reassurance about the importance of her role. She was being offered the opportunity to participate in planning what services she would need to help her. Clearly, though, there was something very much amiss.

It was only after a long conversation and a great deal of reassurance that she was able to tell me that she had been sexually abused by her father over a prolonged period when she was less than ten years old. She had learned somehow to cope with the memories. She had a reasonably happy and stable marriage and grown-up children. She had never told anyone about the abuse. Now all her distress was coming to the surface again, since she was being expected to care for the man who had abused her. She had felt completely unable to share this terrible secret with the doctors or anyone else, yet of course she felt totally incapable of becoming her father's carer. She would not give me her name, but I hope very much that, after we had talked, she would have felt able to talk to at least one member of the hospital staff, and I am sure she would have received an understanding reaction. This case sticks in my memory because it was the first, but it is certainly not the only time I have come across this situation.

Carers frequently complain of being ignored by professionals.

Advice from professionals, what's that?

The district nurse comes once a week to bath my mother. I told her every time how difficult it was and once I broke down, but she patted my arm and told me I was a good girl and that I should carry on.

No one has ever asked me if I can cope. I just have to get on with it.

The frustration which carers feel at being ignored, and their despair, is captured in this letter from a woman in her 50s who is looking after her 87-year-old mother.

I have looked after my mother for the last five years through increasing senile dementia. The consequences have included a dramatic deterioration in my health and considerable problems with my employment. I have a senior position in investment banking. It is essential for me to continue working until 60 if I am to get a reasonable pension. I have come close to losing my job because of conflict of interests and I have certainly been passed over for promotion because of my difficulties.

I get by (just) with expensive help from a generous, kind and efficient lady, which enables me to get to work on two days and to work at home for three. I can only just afford this, what with the cost of extra heating and so on.

The reaction of 'professionals' to my situation has been horrendous in its lack of interest. It is universally assumed that I can cope. This includes the assumption that I can take time off work to take my mother to various medical appointments and to be present when various professional 'helpers' call.

I have tried to explain my problems at work and my health problems to the social worker, but she said happily that I am not the patient. The hypocrisy and cant are unbelievable.

My mother was offered a place at a local Day Centre one or two days a week. This involved her being picked up at 9 a.m. and sitting in a cold bus or ambulance for an hour. She was the first to be collected and the last to be brought back. She returned at 4 p.m. The social worker could not understand that this was of no help to either of us. My mother was always complaining of being cold, and in vain did I point out that my working day actually began at 7 a.m., when I leave to catch my train, and lasts until 7 p.m., when I return. I also pointed out that in order to get her to go the Day Centre I had to cope with two or three hours of argument and pleas for her to get dressed so she would be ready in time. No understanding or suggestions of help have been given to me, except that the social services lady suggested I should have a crisis and then they would do something. She did not specify what sort of crisis. I have told the GP and the social worker that I have come close to hitting my mother and that I am fearful that I will do so one day. Their reaction is silence.

The waiting list for the local home is two years. I asked for some help in finding and assessing a private home, in case I needed mother to go in one, possibly if I was ill. Help was refused. I was also told that mother could only go in a private home if I paid the full charges. No information was given me that the DHSS would or could pay part of the fees.

I am in near despair. I feel so isolated, so without help. I have few friends left — after five years of struggling to keep on with my job and cope with mother, I have had little or no time left over for

personal leisure activities, and if I do have some spare time I am
physically and mentally exhausted.

   Sometimes you read advice which tells you not to be afraid to ask
for help and to talk it over with people. All I can say is that people
who give such advice don't live in the real world, at least not round
here.

This carer tried, didn't she? Told by the social worker to
have a crisis, she told people that she was afraid of hitting
her mother, and what happened? She was still ignored.
Perhaps the sort of crisis that was meant was actually hitting her mother or even doing her an injury.

They may feel Guilty about Them

In Chapter 3, I wrote about the guilt feelings of carers, and
how these inform and influence their behaviour. It is, I
think, an interesting phenomonon that professionals who
work with carers often mirror this reaction. As carers themselves seem to feel that, whatever they do for the cared-for
person, it is never enough, so there is a sense in which
professionals feel that they too can never do enough for
carers.

   I can't help it, whenever I'm with a carer I feel so bloody guilty.
It's as though I'm the most privileged person I know, and I know
that nothing I can do for them will ever get away from the fact that I
can go home and leave the situation, and that's the one thing they
can't do, not ever. It's a huge power they've got over you. A social
worker

The atmosphere between carers and professionals
seems, almost inevitably, to be one of suspicion and mistrust. This is apparent when you have experiences of trying
to work with carers and professionals together. For
example, the professionals will often be very loath to work
in a group in which carers are present. As one doctor put it:

   I'm quite willing to discuss the problems we have in the practice,
and even my own personal problems, in front of my own col-

leagues. But to do so in front of patients or their carers, who are often also my patients, is another thing. How will they accept my diagnosis another time if they have heard me bleating on about my inadequacies? I defy any professional to feel happy about doing that, however much they want to help carers.

It is probably not surprising that some professionals feel like this. Many of them, perhaps the majority, will be people who chose that particular profession because they were caring and compassionate and wanted to do something to help other people. Indeed, they are often referred to as 'carers' themselves, or at least as the 'caring professions'. The use of the word carer to mean these professionals has caused some dismay among family carers, if only because it has led to the use of the term 'informal' carer for the family carer, which many of them dislike heartily.

So the professional carers feel guilty if, because of a shortage of resources, they cannot help as much as they might want to. They feel guilty, too, because, at the the end of the day, they themselves can go home, leaving the carer in a situation from which she has no escape. It is this feeling which also tends to lead to the situation I mentioned above, where the professional does not ask the question because he or she is afraid of hearing what the answer will be, of being forced to recognise that he cannot help. We should perhaps be asking questions about the training of professionals, or indeed about their working situations, which lead them to see themselves in the role of provider, or make them believe they have to be able to make everything better.

There is also a tendency among some professionals to see the carer in rather idealised terms, as some kind of angel, constantly subordinating her own needs to those of the person for whom she is caring. This, too, creates difficulties in communication and may make it hard for the carers to confess their own anxieties and fears to the professionals, in case they disillusion them. Angela, who is looking after her husband who has Parkinson's disease, recalls her feelings.

My social worker was such a lovely lady. She was so kind and understanding to me and always made time, even though I know she was so busy. She always said how much she admired the way I coped, and that meant a lot to me. But somehow I felt she sort of gave me credit for what I was not, if you know what I mean. She seemed to feel I was always patient with him, whereas I knew I shouted sometimes. Even though she kept saying she understood how difficult it must be for me, I felt I shouldn't really say about the shouting. One day, I even pushed him over when he was being especially awful, but when Pat (the social worker) came the next week I didn't mention it. I suppose I thought it would make her think less of me and I didn't want that.

These feelings of guilt are not only aroused by carers. Social workers, health workers and many others may feel that they live in a permanent state of siege from the media and the public, almost never praised and rarely recognised (again, just like carers, perhaps?). It must seem as though they are constantly criticised and never acknowledged. I was not therefore entirely surprised by the reaction of one community psychiatric nurse recently, when I was doing a seminar. I showed a video film of what carers are going through — a film which is usually moving to professionals, though carers themselves seem to think it doesn't show their situation to be anything like as bad as it is in reality. At the end of the film there was silence, punctuated by discreet sniffles from the audience, because the last case study was particularly moving. Suddenly, a nurse at the back stood up and said:

'I'm absolutely sick of being bombarded by people like you with this sort of thing. Can't you, for heaven's sake, start showing us examples of where it works well, where carers are being helped, instead of all this guilt stuff?'

There was a mixed reaction in the room — some of her colleagues agreed with her but the majority did not. After a long discussion, most seemed to agree that the reason why she had made the remark was the most important thing. It had come from her deep sense of inadequacy about ever being able to do enough to help carers. Sometimes the only way people can deal with emotions which are that strong is to become angry about them. Some become angry with the system, with their bosses, with the government, some with people who are giving seminars.

They may be Impatient with Them

About once a week at least, I receive an anguished phone call from a social worker, volunteer organiser or health worker. 'I can't understand it,' they say. 'Where are all the carers who are so desperate for help?' It usually turns out that they have set up some sort of scheme for helping carers, sometimes at considerable cost, both financially and personally, in getting it off the ground. What happens then is that no carers appear to want to take advantage of it. The following story is typical.

A small group of professionals who work with carers make an application for some Joint Funding money. This is a special 'pot' of money for joint ventures between health and social services. They are very concerned that carers are taking responsibility for some heavily dependent people and wish to use the money to help the carers. They decide that what is needed is a scheme to relieve carers when they want to have a break. Accordingly, they recruit and train a group of volunteers who will be substitute carers, just paid their expenses, not for their time. They advertise the scheme in the local paper and are very disappointed when only ten enquiries are received. Four of these are from people who wish to train as substitute carers and two are from handicapped people living alone. Of the remaining four, two carers say that they are 'only enquiring', two more say they will give it a try. Not unnaturally, the professionals are a little miffed that their best efforts appear to be going so badly awry, especially in view of the guilt they always feel about not doing enough.

In my experience there are generally two specific reasons why this lack of take-up occurs.

First, the professionals have either not sufficiently researched the needs of the carers in their area, or they have
researched them with the wrong people. They may have
asked doctors or other professionals what carers want, but
not the carers themselves, and therefore their assumptions
are incorrect. In saying this I must acknowledge how difficult it is actually to consult carers: even if you say you have
been in touch with them, there will be people who say you
have consulted the wrong ones. The needs of the most
accessible carers, for example, perhaps those who go to a
carers group, may not be the same as the need of those who
never come into contact with anyone. We cannot ask for
more than a genuine attempt at consultation or research.
This 'rush to relief' on the part of some professionals is
entirely understandable. Filled with guilt about not doing
enough for carers, they may feel very anxious to get *something* going, no matter what, so that the next time a survey,
an enquiry or a carers group asks them for details of their
provision for carers, their response can be positive.

The second reason for lack of take-up seems to me more
important and significant: carers appear to have great difficulty in accepting any kind of help for themselves, and this
reluctance can make them a frustrating group of people to
deal with. As a society we find it difficult to confront the
issue of mutual dependence — the fact that the carer may
become as dependent on the cared-for person as the latter is
on her — and it is not easy to work with an individual who
cannot accept that all relationships are two-way streets.
The carer may badly wish for the freedom to go out one
afternoon per week, but given that freedom, how is she to
use it? If she has lost all her friends she may have no one to
go with, no longer have any interests that she wishes to
pursue. All that may be understandable. But the carer may
actually fear that if someone else comes into the house and
takes over her role, even for a short time, she may find that
she herself is less indispensable than she thought. We all
want to be needed and may feel perversely pleased when

we feel that we are irreplaceable, however overburdened it makes us. Every parent will recognise the vaguely 'put out' feeling which comes over you when you return after leaving a crying child to be told by a smug grandparent, 'Oh, he stopped crying as soon as you were out of the door,' or, 'I can't think why you say he's so difficult to get off to sleep, he was a little angel every night.' As parents we learn to live with that, but many professionals find the same attitudes hard to accept in carers.

Is this because of the guilt those who work with carers feel? As the carer's feeling of guilt at not doing enough often gets in the way of her accepting help, does the professional's guilt about not doing enough also get in the way of understanding this perfectly natural emotion?

If so, what can we do about it? Well, clearly the most effective way would be to improve the understanding between carers and professionals. When I am involved in training professionals I quite often use a role-play in which a group discussion is taking place. Some of the people taking part play roles which are familiar to them, although not always in their own immediate experience — such as a Director of Social Services or a comunity psychiatric nurse — while two members of the group are given roles as carers. The task of the group is to allocate a gift of money in some way, to provide much-needed relief for carers. It is astonishing how often the role-play develops in the same way — denying the carers a say in how the money is spent, and certainly not allowing them to participate fully as members of the group and to make their needs known. Those professionals who are playing the role of carer are frequently amazed at how powerless they feel and how patronised by the other members of the group. And this is from professionals who are committed to working with carers and are in touch with their problems, otherwise they would not be on the training course at all!

What lies behind this difficulty in understanding between professionals and carers? I would cite three main problems: lack of knowledge, stereotyped images and the imbalance of power between the two groups.

LACK OF KNOWLEDGE

If you are in the business of delivering services or administering any kind of social welfare, it is likely that you will have no difficulty in recognising the initials CPN, FPC, DoH, SSD (for the record: community psychiatric nurse, Family Practitioner Committee, Department of Health, Social Services Department). If you are a carer, it is highly unlikely that you will know any of them. The system is complex enough for those who work in it but virtually impossible to understand if you are encountering it for the first time.

Recently I sat in a government department with a carer who showed from something she said that she did not understand one of the most basic, if not *the* most basic fact about our social welfare system — that Health Service funding comes entirely from central government, while social services funding comes partly from the local rates and is administered by the Local Authority. Shocked looks were exchanged by the civil servants present, at this basic lack of knowledge, but after all, why *should* the carer know?

Carers simply cannot distinguish between all the different people who may be involved in the systems, let alone sort out the vagaries of the boundaries between them.

What I can't understand is how they sort of fit together. The DHSS and Social Services seem to be the same to me, but when you talk to one lot they don't seem to know who you are talking about if you mention the folks in the other office.

If lack of knowledge is a problem, so is the assumption of knowledge which carers do not in fact have. This may be particularly apparent when professionals assume that carers know how to do certain things.

I had been a medical secretary both in hospital and in general practice, and for some reason this meant that people assumed I knew what to do in ALL circumstances and no one offered me any help. When my father had impacted faeces, due to the drugs he was taking, I had to evacuate his rectum manually. This, as you can imagine, was very distressing and embarrassing for my hitherto very fastidious and modest father, and not very pleasant for me. When I asked for help I was given some micro-enemas, but absolutely no instruction in how to use them.

Professionals may also assume knowledge in carers about the course and progress of an illness. Carers often mention being very frightened by an incident such as, say, a handicapped child having some kind of fit, only to have a professional say afterwards, 'Oh yes, that's very common, there is nothing to worry about.' Not unnaturally, the carer thinks that if it is so common, it is a pity no one bothered to mention it before!

So why did no one mention it? Probably for the very best of intentions. The professional will say that, as the fits do not *always* happen, there is no point in worrying the carer unnecessarily; whereas the carer may well feel that the knowledge would have helped her greatly had she had it at the time.

STEREOTYPED IMAGES

Earlier in this chapter I mentioned the images which professionals have of carers, but that applies in reverse also. The carer may feel awe, fear or mistrust, and although these emotions may have absolutely nothing to do with the actual people she is dealing with, they may have a great deal to do with the images she has developed about what people in particular professions are *expected* to be like. We all know, for example, that a general practitioner is a very wise but busy man whose time we do not want to waste; that a nurse is very overworked and underpaid, and that a social worker is either a left wing intellectual who wishes to empower the working classes, or a controlling snooper

who wants to take every child away from its family. Exag-
gerations, perhaps, but clearly we do carry images like
these around in our heads. So firmly fixed are they in many
instances, that even a different experience makes them
hard to shift.

*The doctor called to see my mother last week. He asked her how
she was and if she was eating and sleeping all right. He stayed
about ten minutes, I suppose. He said he thought she was absolutely fine and not a bit confused. As soon as he'd gone my mother
asked if he was the milkman and why he hadn't collected the
money! Still, if he says she's not confused I suppose he knows, and
anyway, he hasn't got the time to keep coming here, I'm sure he's
got worse people to see.*

These stereotyped attitudes exist not only between carers
and professionals, but also between the professionals
themselves. I have never yet sat in on a professional group
which did not moan about the lack of availability of the GP.
In the role-play I mentioned above, the person who is given
the role of the GP almost invariably looks at his or her watch
half-way through, announces that he or she is busy, and
withdraws! In turn, GPs think social workers never do
anything practical, while social workers think that health
workers do not understand the emotional problems of their
clients. All these images are easy to refute in individual
cases, but the myths persist.

How can the images be changed? I believe the only real
way is by replacing them with positive ones. And how can
this happen? Surely it is only possible through *good* experiences and through training. Knowing each other better and
understanding each other's points of view can bring about
changes, although it may be necessary to be patient.
Changing attitudes takes time!

IMBALANCE OF POWER

Imagine the scene: a carer rings up the doctor's surgery
when she is at the end of her tether. She wants to make an

appointment to see the doctor about how she is feeling. Specifically, she wants to discuss with him the possibility of having her husband, who is suffering from Parkinson's disease, cared for elsewhere for a short time while she gets a break. The telephone is answered by the receptionist and the conversation goes like this:

Dr B's surgery.
Yes, I'd like to make an appointment to see the doctor.
Is it for yourself?
Well, not exactly.
Oh, who is it for?
It's about my husband.
Ah yes, Mrs A. Do you need a new prescription?
Not exactly.
Do you need the doctor to call?
Not really, you see it's about a break for me.
How can doctor help?
Well I don't know, I thought perhaps . . .
I see your husband has an appointment booked for next month, hasn't he? Do you want it brought forward?
No, it's more I wanted to talk about —
Doctor's a very busy man, you know.
Yes. I'm sorry to have troubled you.

The receptionist no doubt has the best of intentions. She sees her job as having to sort out the patients who genuinely (in her view) need the doctor's attention, in order to ration his precious time. No doubt, too, if the carer insists on seeing the doctor and is able clearly to articulate what she wants, the appointment will be made. But the carer is not able to insist because she has the greatest difficulty in even beginning to admit that her needs are in any way legitimate. She simply feels powerless and has no strength to join battle with the receptionist.

I get quite a lot of hassle with the doctor's receptionist. Especially when I try to book an ambulance to take Mother to the hospital for her appointments. She is always telling me that ambu-

lances cost £120 and it makes me feel terrible, so I've stopped asking now and I pay for a taxi.

Similarly, the carer who is invited to the case conference, to discuss the discharge of her mother, is not feeling the equal of the staff there. They are speaking in jargon she does not understand, even though they are being nice to her and saying that they want her opinions.

It wasn't that they were horrible to me or anything, on the contrary they couldn't have been nicer. The doctor even got up and brought my coffee to me, and they kept saying that I was the most important person in the equation and in the package of care they were going to put on for Mother. But I don't know what an equation is, to be honest, or a package of care, come to that. I just didn't feel I could say how frightened I was. I would have sounded so feeble and somehow ungrateful. That's odd, really, because they all kept saying how grateful they were to me!

Because the professionals have a monopoly of the jargon and often a monopoly of the information too, and because the carer, due to her own images of professionals, may be reluctant to challenge or even question them, it is perhaps not surprising that the power in the relationship is so un-evenly distributed. I should emphasise that keeping the power in their own hands may not be intentional on the part of the professionals. They may genuinely believe that the carers are better off not knowing about the course of the illness; often they are genuinely trying to enable the carer to participate equally.

The balance can be evened up by improving the carers' confidence in themselves. Ways of doing this, and other ways of improving the relationships between carers and professionals, will be considered in the next chapter.

6   What Makes it Bearable?

In Chapter 1 I outlined the problems carers have in three main areas: financial, practical and emotional. So far, much of this book has concentrated on discussing these problems, but in this chapter I shall consider ways in which the caring situation can be made easier or more bearable. I shall look at actual experiences which have helped carers and indicate *why* these schemes or ideas have been helpful both to carers and those who work with them.

From my own work with carers, it seems to me that help for them comes in three main ways: first, by recognising that they *are* carers and that they have legitimate needs; secondly, by giving them access to some sort of relief or respite; and thirdly, by giving them emotional support in the work they do.

GETTING IN TOUCH

Carers are a hidden group; as I said in Chapter 1, we do not really know how many there are. They are isolated. The word 'carer' is not known to most people, and their needs are usually subordinated to those of the person they are looking after. So schemes for getting in touch with them usually have to be original and innovative. Such a scheme was the Rochdale Carers' Charter.

In 1986, the secretary of the Rochdale Branch of the National Council for Carers and their Elderly Dependants went to a seminar organised by Age Concern, about 'ageing well'. She wondered whether it would be possible to put on a similar kind of event to help carers. She approached the local Health Education Authority, which agreed to help organise a 'Carers' Day'. A planning group was formed, consisting of carers, local politicians, and representatives from health services, social services and the voluntary sector.

The first problem they tackled was how to get in touch with carers. They decided on a four-pronged strategy. First, they decided to approach the Post Office to see if information about the Carers' Day could be distributed with pensions and allowances. Owing to various complicated regulations, this process was fraught with difficulties. Although the spirit of the individual counter clerks was more than willing, the flesh of the bureaucracy was weak, and although several hundred slips advertising the day were supplied to post offices, only about twenty new contacts with carers resulted. But, as the organisers said, 'We were grateful if *any* carer found out about us.'

Next, a publicity campaign was set in motion. Posters were produced and press releases sent to local papers. The organisers were disappointed when few carers contacted them directly via this route, but felt it was particularly useful in raising awareness among professionals, who in turn passed the information on to carers.

The third and most effective approach proved to be through the primary health care teams — doctor's surgeries, health centres and District and Community Nurses. A leaflet was produced and circulated to all these outlets, and to the Community Nurse Education Department. Doctors were asked to discuss the day with the staff in their practices, and to alert receptionists to the fact that patients might be seeking information about it. Posters and leaflets were supplied to waiting areas, and nurses were keen to distribute these to people whose homes they were visiting.

The fourth arm of the publicity campaign was the planning group itself, through their own networks, and through contacts such as Community Health Councils, Well Women's clinics and social services departments. Because this group had worked with carers and because the carers themselves were involved with the planning, they recognised that it was difficult to overcome the feelings of guilt carers have at the thought of doing anything for themselves. They therefore decided to concentrate the day on carers' health needs. They reckoned that carers would more readily accept a day which focused on health needs, rather than on any other kind of support. 'We thought carers would feel that if they kept healthy, it would help them care better, so that would be acceptable to them,' said one of the organisers.

When the day came, it was attended by 150 carers, far more than the organisers had anticipated. The programme began at noon, in order to give carers a free morning to cope with their caring duties. People were invited to bring their own lunch and to chat with the organisers and with other carers. Tea and coffee were supplied. After a brief introduction to the aims of the day, participants were invited to join smaller groups or workshops, which had very specific aims: to give carers an opportunity to air their health problems and to hear what statutory and voluntary help was on offer. There were four workshops, and details had been given about them in the earlier publicity to help the participants choose. The workshops were:

Stress
Carers are extremely vulnerable in terms of mental health. Stress involves severe emotional strain, worry, depression, anxiety and physical illness. Fatigue and sleeplessness are almost universal problems among carers. Do we recognise stress when we experience it? What are crisis points? Can it be prevented? What help is available? What is the role of medication?

Family Relationships
Carers may experience illness as a result of a close relationship which involves relentless caring. They may also find

themselves at the sharp end of conflicts between spouses, children and relatives. What family pressures put carers at risk? How can they be prevented? What help is available?

Women's Health Needs
Many carers are under pressure at a time when their own health as women may be creating new problems, but the stresses of their role may mean that they delay getting health care and advice, especially for problems connected with menstruation or the menopause. What is the relationship between stress and these problems? What is the role of the Health Services? Who can help prevent illness?

Help for Health and How to Get it
Some carers are well aware of both their health problems and their health needs, but how do they get help? What is the role of health counselling, screening and positive health checks? Does your doctor understand your problems? What can you do for yourself?

The organisers described the reactions of the carers who attended the day as 'extraordinary'. The group sessions produced a wealth of information about the stress of caring and about carers' anxieties and fears. The opportunity to talk, even briefly, about these problems was very much valued, as was the opportunity for carers and professionals to talk together. Most of all, however, the carers seemed to feel that because someone had taken the trouble to focus on them for an afternoon, they could much more freely admit their own needs and legitimately ask for things for themselves and for services to help them. Up to 100 carers emerged 'from the woodwork', as one nurse said, about whom no one had previously had any information.

The outcome of this day was that a Carers' Charter was produced, setting out a variety of ways in which health and welfare services could help. It stressed the need for consultation and communication with carers, to improve their access to services. It also pointed out that its recommendations did not on the whole mean more expenditure because they were aware of the local constraints on finance. The publication of the charter brought more publicity, and that in turn meant that more carers were able to get in touch and make their needs known.

A different approach was taken by the organiser of a care attendant scheme in Evesham. Still aimed at enabling carers to get in touch with someone who could help them, the focus of this day was on marshalling potentially helpful organisations to put on a 'Carers' Fair', with stands and exhibitions displaying what was available in the area.

The event was widely publicised. Thousands of leaflets were distributed door-to-door, and home helps also agreed to give them to their clients. Posters and leaflets were displayed in surgeries and local libraries. The local papers interviewed a number of carers and the local radio station advertised the event. The chosen venue was a day centre and money was raised by writing to local charities and to the Town Council, asking each for a set donation of £25. All but one responded. An invitation to take part was sent to all relevant local organisations, ranging from small self-help groups and local societies to larger, nationally known voluntary associations and statutory services. Each participating local organisation was given a dislay board and a table.

As well as the exhibitions, three sessions of special interest to carers were timetabled into the day. These were on 'Care at Home', 'Looking After Yourself' and 'Welfare Benefits'. Experts ran these sessions and the carers could listen and ask questions. Videos by various organisations were also shown. Unlike the Rochdale event, where carers were expected to come alone, the Evesham scheme encouraged the person being cared for to come too. A quiet area was provided, where elderly people could sit while their carers went round the stalls, and toys from a toy library and video films were supplied for handicapped children and their brothers and sisters. The attendance at the event was remarkable: people travelled long distances in order to attend, and the organisers were delighted at the number of people who seemed to benefit. Many of the carers who came had had no idea of the range of allowances they could claim, and many more had never heard of the local schemes available to help them.

Both the above events aimed to try to get in touch with as many carers as possible, with the aim of making them more aware of what was available to them; other schemes may concentrate more on giving carers the opportunity to talk to professionals who may not always understand their problems.

A group of professionals who are particularly important to carers are General Practitioners. As part of a King's Fund research project whose aim was to improve the relationship between GPs and carers, the MSD Foundation held a series of six workshops in selected places in England and Scotland. Carers, GPs, consultants from nearby hospitals, social workers and District Nurses were invited to an evening meeting. Supper was provided so that the participants could spend time talking together before the 'business' part of the evening. This began with everyone watching a video of two interviews with carers. The meeting then split into two groups of eight people, evenly divided by profession and, of course, including carers. The groups then spent an hour trying to identify the needs of carers and the key issues which would enable the doctors and other professionals to provide better support for them.

All participants felt that the workshops had been enjoyable and helpful, and the professionals especially thought that having the carers present had been extremely important. Without them, it would have been too easy to assume that services were being satisfactorily provided, and to seek refuge in phrases like, 'Of course families must look after their elderly and disabled relatives; if they don't, who will?' Through talking to the carers, the professionals became more aware of the latters' views and of their reluctance to bother professionals, especially GPs, whom they regarded as far too busy to listen to their problems. The professionals felt reassured by how little the carers seemed to want — they wanted GPs to recognise the work they were doing and the strain they were under, and they wanted regular home visits without having to ask for them. They also realised how little information the carers had and how lost they felt about where they could turn for help. From the nurses, the carers wanted instruction in practical skills like lifting, and from social workers they wanted information about equipment, financial help and respite care.

According to the questionnaires which they filled in at the end of the sessions, the professionals went away from the workshops keen to examine their current practice and to make changes which would better accommodate the needs of carers. Some also wanted to set up more workshops in order to spread the message among colleagues. The carers went away feeling extremely pleased to have been consulted and glad to have been able not only to put their point of view, but to have it listened to. As one put it:

I almost didn't go because I'm not used to speaking up in a group and especially with it being doctors, I thought I'd be too nervous to say anything. But when I got there I realised that they did want to hear what I had to say, in fact they'd come to learn from me. For the first time in years I felt as though someone felt that my opinion counted for something. I went home feeling ten feet tall.

Other Ways of Getting in Touch

Using the Media
Sometimes those of us working with carers despair of ever being able to make contact with as many as we would like. In itself, caring isolates people, and although the examples given above enabled carers to express their views in various ways, there is always the feeling that for every carer who does get in touch, there are dozens, perhaps hundreds, who do not. Nothing brings this home more than the ex-

perience of carers' organisations following a radio or TV
broadcast. From the moment the programme ends their
switchboards are jammed, and there is a huge increase in
mail over the next few days. Indeed, when I am appearing
on TV it is not unusual for the calls to my colleagues in the
office to begin before the programme has even finished.
The letters and phone calls which come in after such broad-
casts have a common theme. They all say something like:

*I had no idea I was a carer and that there were so many people
doing what I'm doing. When I heard/saw the item I realised you
were talking about me. I didn't know there was any help for people
like me. Do you think I would be able to get ... Invalid Care
Allowance, a sitting service, an incontinence service, some adaptations to my home?...'*

Articles or letters about carers in local and national newspapers are also good ways to get in touch, although they
don't have the immediate power and impact of radio and
TV.

This kind of publicity poses problems for carers' organisations. We want very much to get in touch with as many
carers as possible, but a mention in the media strains our
limited staff and our scarce resources to the utmost, in
terms of the time which must be spent dealing with the
resulting queries.

Carers' Centres

Some areas have experimented with a 'one stop' centre
where carers can go for information. There is one in
Cheshire, for example, which is open every day of the week
— from 9.30 a.m. to 9.30 p.m. on weekdays, and shorter
hours at the weekends. It employs two full-time workers
and 12 ancillary workers on a shift basis. It is well publicised
and carers are encouraged to drop in for a chat. Staff are
always available to discuss problems and to refer carers to
other agencies. Many local professionals are interested in
the centre and welcome referrals of carers who are in need

of help. There is a strong emphasis on confidentiality. As well as providing information, the centre gives practical help in the form of an incontinence laundry service. It also serves as a meeting place for carers, where they can share their problems if they feel so inclined.

There are several reasons why the above ways of getting in touch with carers have been successful. They have been innovative in the way they have approached the problem — trying new ideas and methods and, on occasion, not being afraid to use a 'hard sell' approach. But they have also made use of existing channels and relationships in order to build on them and use them in fresh ways. Above all, they have succeeded in convincing carers that what they were being offered was worthwhile and would be of help. All too frequently, carers feel that it is not worth bothering to try to make their needs known. Convincing them that their needs *are* worth bothering about is the most effective way of encouraging them to come forward.

Getting Relief

'Time off' and 'time to be myself' are some of the most important needs which carers express. As we saw in Chapter 2, respite care can be provided in a number of different ways: it can be in the home or outside it; it can be regular or sporadic. The following are several examples of what respite care can mean for carers, and some different ways in which it can be provided.

There is a club in West London which aims to enhance the quality of life for older Afro-Caribbean people by providing recreation, companionship, support and advice. It is open five days a week from 9.30 a.m. to 4 p.m. A meal is provided at lunchtime, as well as various activities such as drawing, rugmaking and picture framing. Some of the people who attend are living alone, but many are also being looked after by a carer. Knowing that the elderly person for whom they are responsible can be happily and sometimes productively occupied in the centre is very reassuring for carers and enables them to do their shopping, keep their appointments, or just sleep for the afternoon in peace.

In Scotland, a Sitter Service, set up in 1983, caters for single parents with handicapped children and for carers looking after frail elderly people. A sitter goes to a family free of charge for periods of up to four hours at any one time, although this does not include overnight sitting. Four paid sitters are available, but they are supported by a strong force of over 60 volunteers. One of the mothers who uses the service describes it thus:

The Sitter Service has completely transformed our lives. The relief of being able to have just one night out in the week — it's indescribable.

This mother has three children with the same disability, a rare form of muscular dystrophy. They are aged 8, 7 and 4, and since they were born the household has been, according to their mother, 'complete pandemonium'. With the help of the Sitter Service, she and her husband are able to cope more efficiently with all the demands on their time and energy. Every Sunday evening, a sitter arrives to look after the three children while the parents are free to visit friends, go to the cinema or out for a meal. The time is precious to the couple, because it enables them to relax together and gather strength for the week ahead. The service is very much in demand, too, for single parents, some of whom have not been out for months or even years. The organiser says:

The kind of families who apply to us are often ones who haven't got family or friends nearby. Also they don't want to ask friends or family to make a regular commitment —like once a week while they go to an evening class — because it's a lot to ask and they know they can't reciprocate. Single parents cannot, after all, leave their children to go and look after someone else's. Someone who has volunteered to sit for them because they want to is a different story and easier to accept.

The volunteers in the project are as wide-ranging as their many skills, and the project leaders find that an unusual volunteer can be matched to an unusual family. They are found through a campaign that usually attracts between 12 and 20 people, about three quarters of whom will normally be acceptable. Potential volunteers attend a series of three evening meetings which give them an opportunity to learn from the previous experience of other volunteers. They will then be interviewed by the project leader and their references taken up. Their expenses are reimbursed. The volunteers find the work very satisfying, partly because they can actually gauge an improvement in the life-style of the carer. One volunteer reported that when he first started sitting for a single mother with two children, she was very overweight and uninterested in her appearance. She had not been out since her separation a year earlier. After the volunteer had been sitting for six months, he noticed a remarkable change. She had lost weight and cared a great deal more about how she looked, but more importantly, she had developed the self-confidence to go out alone when friends were not available.

A Crossroads Care scheme was introduced to help the parents of mentally handicapped children in the Wirral. Ten families, each with a severely mentally handicapped child, were chosen to take part in a pilot project in which a trainee care attendant was provided regularly. In addition to the continual care requirements and physical strain of looking after a severely handicapped child, the families found that the obsessive behaviour of the children, their lack of communication, and the need for constant thinking ahead and for concentrating on providing a safe environment, caused great strain on family and marriage relationships. Although some of the parents had been able to arrange the very occasional night out together, the anxiety they experienced while they were out, and the obligation they felt to see to all the child's needs beforehand, made it difficult for them to relax and enjoy themselves.

When the offer of Crossroads support was made to them, several families had some reservations and felt it was 'too good to be true, there must be a catch somewhere'. The main reservations were whether the care attendant would be able to cope with the child's behaviour and personal needs; how well the child would get on with the care attendant, and whether the child would take to the care attendant. After an introductory visit, eight of the ten families felt confident in the care attendant's ability to cope with any eventuality and were satisfied by the relationship which had been established with the child. It was five to six weeks before one family left the child alone with the care attendant, and before another carer felt that she did not have to deal with the child's personal care before she went out.

Several of the carers confessed to the dilemma they had suffered in deciding how much they should reveal to the scheme co-ordinator and the prospective care attendant, especially if the child had anti-social habits or problems associated with adolescence. They did not want to put the care attendant off, or hinder their chance of receiving help, and yet they felt that the care attendant should be fully aware of all the difficulties which might arise.

The main effect of the Crossroads relief was that the parents could begin to develop a life of their own together, and this stimulated a new interest in living, in their marriage and in their home. Instead of automatically declining invitations, they could say 'perhaps' and make a commitment to attend something regularly. They could now actually relax and enjoy themselves while they were out, because they were confident in the ability of the substitute carer to cope. They found the scheme entirely reliable: the attendant would always arrive punctually and they knew she would be able to deal with any unexpected circumstances; and it was flexible, too: they could receive help at the time they needed it. One mother spoke about her feelings:

If parents can have time off and families have an outing, without the handicapped child but knowing that he or she is well cared for by a care attendant, this could well contribute towards happier marital relationships. Time given is not just valuable for its practical purpose but also makes the family feel that somebody cares and that they have the support of the outside world.

My daughter now attends a special school, so I decided that I would take a teaching certificate covering further education. The course was held one day a week but overran the time when she was expected home from school. I knew, as she cannot feed herself unaided and is doubly incontinent, that it would be difficult to find someone to take over from me. This was not a job for the social services, and my relatives were unable to assist on account of age, state of health or personal commitments. A Crossroads care attendant now meets her from school, gives her supper and a bath and entertains her until I arrive home. This allows me to have some adult company, which I miss when my husband is away, and to get some useful qualifications.

Some carers can arrange for the person they are caring for to be looked after at home, or to go into residential care, while they themselves have a holiday. For others, however, the best form of respite is to have the home to themselves for a week or so, while the cared-for person goes on holiday. The Parkinson's Disease Society has built up a tradition of organising special holidays for their sufferers. A typical summer programme would include holidays at special centres for the disabled, which offer activities and daily outings; holidays which include music and art therapy; and holidays specially aimed at younger sufferers, which include yoga, meditation and visualisation sessions. The holidays are not confined to the United Kingdom and sufferers have the opportunity to go abroad also. On some of the holidays, carers are encouraged to go also if they wish, but a large number are specifically designed to give carers and cared-for time apart from each other. Financial help is available where the family cannot meet the cost out of their own resources.

These respite care schemes are all very different from each other, but they have certain key elements in common. Firstly, they are accessible to the carer, because they are acceptable to the cared-for person. In a sense, respite schemes are dependent on the willingness of the cared-for person to take advantage of them. Second, the schemes meet the needs of the cared-for person as well as those of the carer. Many carers are put off the idea of taking up some form of respite placement because they feel that the person they are looking after will not be happy — a young person in a geriatric ward, for example, or an elderly person who is physically handicapped in a ward or home with elderly mentally infirm people.

Thirdly, the schemes show that any relief offered to carers must be sensitive to their needs and flexible enough to take account of them. This means that the organisers must be prepared to consult with carers, to listen to what they say and to change what is on offer if it does not seem to meet their needs. Take, for example, the scheme for a sitting service for the elderly mentally infirm, which was set up in Yorkshire. The scheme had two paid co-ordinators whose job was to:

* Work closely with Health Centre staff in promoting the project and establishing relationships with local voluntary and statutory agencies.
* Make contact with households containing an elderly confused person and offer support to the carers.
* Recruit and organise a network of volunteers who could be called on to relieve relatives in the day or in the evenings.

The scheme got underway in the spring of 1982. Thirty-six carers were visited, all of whom had been judged by their General Practitioners to be under a high level of stress. Nineteen said they wanted no help at all, and only three wanted a regular sitter. Two and a half years later, 123 carers had been visited and again only a very small minority wanted a regular sitter. It would have been very easy for the organisers to conclude that because of the low take-up of the scheme, the carers they visited had no need of any support. But of course this was not the case. They might not have wished to take up the offer of the sitter, but they had a need for someone who would understand their problems. The project workers always left their telephone number, emphasising that they could be contacted and that they would call again after about a month. The refusal of the relief service did not always mean that the carers were not in need of it, but that they felt unable to take it up at that point. This may have been due to a sense of guilt, reluctance to admit the need for relief, and the reluctance of elderly couples to see themselves as 'carer' and 'dependant'. The organisers of the scheme were willing to accept that they could be offering the 'wrong' service and tried to meet the needs of the carers just by being available. They felt that that of itself lessened the stress for the carer.

Providing support for the carer, then, does not always mean providing respite from the caring role. Other forms of support can be just as valuable.

GETTING SUPPORT

What exactly do we mean when we talk about support? When a carers group was asked in a 'brainstorming' session to define what they meant by support, these are some of the things they wrote:

Understanding
Being valued
Sharing worries
Being listened to
Being heard
Receiving approval
Genuine concern for how I am.

It is interesting to note that there is no mention of practical support in this list. Help with tasks like lifting, dealing with incontinence and aids and adaptations did appear in the list at first, but when the carers in the group were asked to put the long list they had originally produced in order of priority, they agreed the seven items in the above list as the most important. So how do carers receive the kind of support which they identify as being most important? There seem to be three main ways:

By coming to terms with their own feelings.
By being valued by other people.
By feeling that they have some kind of control over their situation.

Coming to Terms with Their Own Feelings

This means that carers are helped to understand that their own feelings are legitimate and, moreover, that they are not alone in feeling them! They may be able to get this support from their own families or within their own neighbourhood. Some may get it from professionals, others may require individual counselling in order to achieve it. For many carers, however, the most effective way is the one that Imogen found, through a carers support group.

I've been looking after my mother-in-law for four years now. She has got Alzheimer's Disease and for about two years hasn't been able to come downstairs at all. She's incontinent, of course, but I cope with that. In fact I cope with most of it, most of the time. But last year I found myself getting impatient with her more often, and I seemed to be losing the sense of humour which I feel is the main thing that pulls you through. For instance, if I take her tea up and she greets me like a stranger and later asks my daughter, 'Who was that woman who just came in?' you've got to laugh, really. But as I say, it was getting me down and really affecting the way I was with my husband. I was feeling —well, it's his mother — why am I the one who is at home clearing up her mess?

I had noticed this poster in the library before, asking for carers to join a new group, but I hadn't taken much notice as I didn't really think of myself as a carer. Then one day I noticed this poster at the doctor's surgery when I was fetching Mum's pills. I had had a particularly trying day with her and I thought I'd just go along to see what it was like. One of the nurses whom I knew was there, and she introduced me to another woman who was caring for a child with spina bifida, and to a man who was looking after his mother who also had Alzheimer's. He mentioned that the old lady often forgot who he was and that it made him feel angry when she did that.

The speaker we had that night was a physiotherapist who told us about lifting. It was quite interesting, but I was more interested in talking to the others, really. They seemed very friendly and there was a lot of comfort in seeing them nod understandingly when I mentioned something that Mum had done. But it wasn't that they moaned on about the people they were looking after. If they'd done that I think I would have felt very disloyal to my family. It was just that they seemed to understand and that made us comrades. One thing I liked was that they seemed to be full of ideas about how the group could help carers — one was planning a coffee morning to raise funds, and others were talking about writing a letter to an MP about some changes in the benefit regulations.

When I went home I felt better than I had been for some time: it was as though I knew that if things were bad at home, I could ring up one of the group and know that no one would look down their nose at me or think less of me because I happened to have been angry with Mum that day. I go to the group regularly, and in fact they've asked me if I'll think about becoming the secretary next year. I've never done anything like that before, but I think I'll take it on. After the group has helped me so much, I feel the least I can do, really, is to give a bit back. If it hadn't been for the group I would never even have applied for the Attendance Allowance or the Invalid Care Allowance. I only did it because they kept asking me how I was getting on with it, and I felt it would be letting them down if I didn't persevere.

Being Valued by Other People

In a society which values people by their success and often by their material achievements, it is easy for carers to feel undervalued. As one put it:

*We haven't yet reached a stage where you can put the word 'carer'
down on a form when you are asked for your occupation.*

The value of the work they do goes largely unacknowledged, so the reaction of other people is crucial, especially
the reactions of professionals. I have mentioned elsewhere
how important it is for the professional to turn to the carers
and ask how *they* are, and it is vital for the carers to feel that
they, as well as the cared-for people, are supported by
involved and caring professionals.

*I know the GP is concerned about me, and so is the occupational
therapist, because they have always insisted that we must get time
off. The nurse always asks me, each time she comes, if I'm all right.
They have really helped me with father because at first he was
pretty unhelpful and seemed to regard everything I did as just my
duty. But the nurse used to make a point of telling him that he was
very lucky to have me looking after him, and always said she was
going to spend some time with me after she had seen to him. When
we got the hoist and the other aids, the nurse told him that it was
for me as well as him, because I was just as important. He seemed
to accept it when the nurse and doctor said it, in a way he never
would have done if it was me saying it.*

*Another marvellous thing about them is that they always insist
that I know best about his condition. When the consultant came to
assess him, my GP came as well and said, 'Now, I'll let Mrs G tell
you all about the patient because she knows more about it than I
do.' It makes you feel that you are doing a job which is worthwhile
and that you count for something.*

Asa, a carer of Asian origin, tells how her situation was
changed by an accidental encounter with a professional
who valued her as a person, not just as a carer:

*When my mother-in-law had gynaecological problems I had of
course to go to the hospital with her because she didn't speak any
English. I didn't mind doing this at all at first, it's only what
anyone would expect to do with a relative. But then it turned out to
be cancer and she was going every week for treatment. I have a good*

*job with the Council and it was getting more and more difficult to
get time off every week to go with her. But naturally it was difficult
to make my family understand this.*

*One day I was having a cup of tea in the tea bar while my
mother-in-law was having her treatment, and I got chatting to this
very nice Asian girl. She was very interested in my problems and
told me she was employed by the Health Authority to work wth
ethnic minority patients and their families. Almost immediately,
or at least that's how it seemed to me, an interpreter appeared in
the clinic, to help women who couldn't speak English, but even
better, they got some kind of scheme going so that these interpreters and other volunteers would meet the patients and sit with them
while they were waiting — in other words, do what I had been
doing for my mother-in-law. By that time her treatment had
finished, so it didn't benefit me or her, but I felt so glad that
someone had listened to me, seen my problem and because of that
managed to help many other people. Most of all, she hadn't just
dismissed it, but taken it seriously and done something about it.*

Feeling in Control of their Situation

Carers are often forced into a system which denies them
any control over their own personal situation. For all of us,
our own internal 'housekeeping' — how we ration what we
give out according to what we have to put in to keep
ourselves going — takes energy. Carers often bankrupt
themselves of energy because they give out so much. Consequently, they cease to have any power over their lives,
because to have power you need energy. If you have no
energy store, you are unlikely to have the strength to in-
dulge in long negotiations with a recalcitrant old person or
a difficult child: you give in and do what they want because
you haven't the energy to do anything else. Similarly, you
need access to information in order to take control of your
life, but if you are physically and mentally exhausted, you
cannot find time to get the information in the first place.
Carers are therefore forced into a 'closed system' with no
support, and the result is they feel trapped and powerless.

Everyone has a point of tolerance beyond which everything breaks down: military personnel are ordered to stop at certain points, airline pilots are strictly forbidden to fly more than a requisite number of hours. Carers can go on until they die.

Flora was such a carer. She is a woman in her forties, caring for her husband who is much older and suffering from Parkinson's Disease. They had in fact been planning to divorce when the Parkinson's diagnosis was made. The house was almost sold and Flora was planning to move back to Devon to be nearer the rest of her family.

When he became ill, I just felt I couldn't leave him in the lurch, but I felt so bad about the way it had happened. I used to tear myself apart thinking, 'If only he hadn't got this terrible illness for another six months.' If I hadn't known about it I wouldn't have had to do anything, and if we had been properly divorced I couldn't have been blamed. Our relationship had been awful for years. There is nearly 25 years between us and it was just too much. He got very bad very quickly and I found there was very little help available. The doctors just assumed I wanted to look after him, and everyone seemed to regard me as a wonderful, selfless, kind person for caring for him. But inside I knew I wasn't, and I lived in an agony of anger and resentment and then terrible guilt. It isn't surprising that I started to be ill myself. I got alopecia and virtually all my hair fell out. I started to have panic attacks and to suffer from insomnia.

At the surgery my doctor finally put me in touch with a counsellor. She was marvellous because for the first time in two years I felt she only wanted to listen to me, and not only did she not ask me about my husband but I felt that she really didn't care about him, only about me. I was able to tell her how I felt my life had got completely out of my control since Jim's illness, and how I felt that no matter what I did, I wouldn't be able to get it back in control, at least not until he was dead. I was even able to tell her how I wished he was dead.

Gradually, and it took several months, I came to see that it was my feelings which were preventing me controlling my own life rather than the circumstances themselves. That freed me to be able to look for some sort of relief for myself. At first I tried the Parkinson's Disease group because I found they had sitters and did holidays, but that didn't suit me because most of the other carers were devoted to the person they were looking after. By now I felt strong enough to admit that I wasn't devoted and that I didn't have to feel guilty about it when, after all, we had been about to be divorced. By now I also felt confident enough to ask for help, and through a social worker I found out that there was a very good private home for patients like Jim. I had never thought of such a thing before, partly because I felt I should look after him myself, but mostly because I felt I should not use our money in that way. His share of our capital was due to his children, I felt. But his son and daughter didn't even visit him, so I realised that the money would be better spent helping him and me. I wish that Jim and I had been able to discuss this, but he is too ill and scarcely knows me most of the time.

What we have now is a satisfactory arrangement where he goes in this care home for two weeks in every four, and stays at home with me for the other two. He seems quite happy and it has made such a difference to me. I can go to stay with friends, or plan a holiday or just stay on my own when he is in the home, and because for two weeks of the month my life is in my own control again. I don't resent the other weeks. It isn't what I planned and we never shall get divorced, but it's bearable and I'm coping. My hair has grown back, too . . .

Support can be given to carers in many different ways, but the most essential ingredient is recognising the value of the carer as a member of society in her own right, cherishing the contribution she makes as a carer, and enabling her to meet her own needs as well as the needs of the person she is looking after.

*   *   *

At the beginning of this chapter, I pointed out that carers have financial problems, practical problems and emotional

problems. We have considered examples of how the latter
two can be addressed, but have not really considered how
the financial problems should be tackled. In the next chapter we shall look at the issue of carers' incomes in more
detail, but we should remember that carers can be helped
financially by ensuring that they claim all the benefits to
which they are entitled. As I mentioned in Chapter 2, these
are inadequate, but even so the take-up of them is low.
Carers are reluctant to claim benefits, they are resistant to
realising that any benefits are available to them, and they
are often put off claiming by the complexities of the system.

A project in Kent was set up to help carers of the elderly
and has laid great emphasis on securing all the benefits to
which carers and the people they care for are entitled. It
offers information and advice to carers about benefits, and
also provides sample letters and is active in helping carers
to process their claims. The project has a team of trained
advocates, experts in the benefit system, who work with
carers and negotiate with the DHSS, pensions systems,
employers and others. Where necessary, bridging loans
can be provided so that the carer can buy in care while
waiting for a claim to be settled. The service is much appreciated by the carers who have taken advantage of it:

*I don't see why anyone else should have the power to decide for
me what I want in the way of services and help. If I have money,
then the power is in my hands and I can buy what I want, to suit
my own situation, not what someone else thinks I should have.
Before I knew about all the benefits, I used to feel apologetic about
money — it didn't seem right somehow to be paid for looking after
someone you love. But now I know I'm entitled to it and, God
knows, I earn every penny.*

7 What Should be Done?

When you sit down with carers, service deliverers and policy makers, as I frequently do, and ask them, 'What should be done for careers?', it is not difficult to get them to arrive at a statement of principles. Broadly, they will say something like this:

We should recognise and acknowledge the contribution made by carers. They should be involved in planning services and be treated as full and equal partners, not as mere recipients of services.

Both carers and cared-for persons should have choice and adequate information on which to base that choice.

Practical help and services should be flexible enough to take account of the differing needs of individuals, including ethical and cultural differences, and they should be available as part of the carer's ordinary life, not simply to meet emergencies at a time of crisis.

Carers should not feel obliged to take on the caring role, but should feel able to say no if they wish.

Carers should have an adequate income and not be penalised financially for taking on the caring task.

Reaching agreement on these principles presents no great difficulties. Turning commitment into reality, however, is often a different matter, as the experiences of carers in this book have shown. This chapter looks at how these principles should be put into practice in order to make life better for carers and for those they care for.

It is interesting (and difficult) to put what carers want and need into some kind of priority order, because there is a sense in which all things mentioned in this chapter are in fact inseparable, and should be thought of as a complete package which would add up to a better deal for carers. But from my everyday contact with carers, and from the experiences of my colleagues, I would suggest the following order of priority:

Carers need **recognition** of what they are doing, of the contribution they are making; they need **respite**, some time to be themselves; they need **information**, both about the disabilities and conditions of the people for whom they are caring and about what is available to help them; they need **practical help** and they need **money**. Let us look at each of these in turn.

RECOGNITION

I must say that, at the carers' day we held, I was really scared of what the carers were going to demand. But what struck me most was just how little *they actually asked for. Basically, it amounted to having us all understand just how much they were doing and for some more understanding of the strain they were under.* A Director of Social Services.

The contribution made by carers to the care and support of elderly people, mentally ill people, mentally handicapped people and those who are disabled, is so massive as to be virtually unmeasurable; yet for years it went almost completely unrecognised, and even now we are only just beginning to acknowledge its size and significance. We have seen that one of the biggest obstacles to recognising the sheer amount of what carers do is that they do not themselves easily appreciate that they are carers, or indeed just what a carer is. In the last chapter we saw some examples of how carers can be helped to get in touch with each other and with helping agencies. How can policymakers and service deliverers recognise better the contribution of carers?

In short, they can try to 'Think Carer'. For too long the presence of a carer in a household was the signal for service deliverers to breathe a sigh of relief and think that that was one problem area they could ignore. The very presence of a carer meant that no extra services were thought necessary, and scarce resources were concentrated on elderly or disabled people who were living alone. There is a conflict in the way carers were and still are expected to carry huge burdens, with their own needs unacknowledged. What policy-makers and service deliverers have to do is make sure that they see the needs of *both* the cared-for person and the carer. The carer needs to feel trusted and valued by professionals and others, and to feel that her needs are being acknowledged also. This means that if she feels she wants to continue working at a much liked or much needed job, that is what she should be helped to do. It is not enough to start from the premise that if the carer gives the job up, *then* help will be provided. It is not for anyone else to make the judgement about whether she should go on working or not: she herself should decide, and support services should be arranged accordingly. The aim should be to work towards partnerships in caring, with the carer being seen as at least an equal partner, not a passive recipient of services.

Local Authorities have a duty to find out about the carers in their area. They should know how many there are and seize every opportunity to get in touch with them. They should use every means at their disposal — from committees, their public relations departments, the local radio — to state explicitly that they want to plan services in partnership with carers, that the presence of a carer is not a reason for refusing or reducing services, and that the level of service provided will be determined in consultation with carers and the person cared for.

These policies should not be confined to services provided in the home, but extended to residential care services also. The aim of these, too, should be to work in part-

nership with carers, so that care in the home and care in a
residential establishment should not be seen as straight
alternatives — you have one *or* the other — but again as
partnerships, whose aim is to provide care in the way
which is best for all concerned. The difficulties in this approach — in trying to resolve the conflicts which may be
inherent in attempting to balance the needs of the cared-for
person, the carer and the resources of the Local Authority,
should be acknowledged and openly discussed and nego-
tiated. This is easier to do once the carer is acknowledged as
a partner, not as a member of another client group. It is true
that if the needs of the carer are not met, she is likely to
become another client or patient, but she should be seen as
a partner in the provision of care, whose opinions and
experiences are at least as important as those of any of the
professionals involved.

General Practitioners should always be aware of the carers' support which is helping their patients, and be prepared to acknowledge the separate needs of the carers,
even though they may know that these raise problems
about the care of their patients.

Carers are not used to being treated as partners, and
most of them find it difficult to cope with the complicated
systems which administer our social services. They may
feel powerless in the face of what they see as bureaucracy,
and before what they feel is the superior knowledge and
experience of their doctor. One way to overcome this may
be to appoint a carers' worker, whose task is to work with
them and on their behalf to raise carers' issues, to get in
touch with them and to help colleagues 'think carer'. Many
areas have experimented in this way and found it
successful.

There is a note of caution to be struck, however. While
the appointment of a carers' worker may be a very good
way of getting the subject 'on the agenda' and of raising
awareness, service providers should be wary of thinking
that, because they have appointed such a worker, they

have done all that is needed. This is no more satisfactory than the situation of a Local Authority which, having appointed an ethnic minority development worker, feels that they have solved their problems. What often happens in that situation is that the workers in the department refer all the 'ethnic minority issues' to that one worker, and nothing is done to help get the needs of ethnic minorities considered by all departments and all workers. Similarly, with a carers' worker, the danger is that if he or she sits on the relevant committees and organises the odd carers' event, policy-makers and service providers will feel they can sit back, secure in the knowledge that the 'carers dimension' has been considered. The aim should be for every department and every worker to have 'Carer' in their minds at all times. A carers' worker can certainly help, but should never be thought of as the complete answer.

It will be clear from the above that there are big implications here for the training of those who work with carers. The fact that at present carers go largely unrecognised owes a great deal to the training of most professionals, which included no reference to them. Agencies should provide training for all their workers — not just social workers but also care assistants, not just GPs but also medical receptionists — in getting in touch with carers, listening to their needs and treating them as partners. They should be trained to recognise the essential differences between the care offered by professionals and that offered by a family member or friend. They should be trained in helping carers to talk through their problems, so that they can be valued by the latter as a listening ear, not necessarily as someone who can solve all their problems; and trained, too, in the skills of negotiating and mediating between the carer and the person cared for. Training policies and policies of career progression in the caring professions should make it clear that skills in sharing with and supporting carers will be valued as highly as skills in diagnosing or supporting those who are dependent.

One of the surest ways to ensure that the contribution of carers is recognised and understood is to involve them not just at the time when services are being delivered, but when they are being planned. 'Why on earth don't they ask us what we want?' is a frequent cry from carers.

How can you get carers to participate in planning? It can be done formally, by ensuring, for example, that carers are represented on all formal planning committees and at all levels. They should have a presence on Joint Consultative Committees (locally based committees made up of representatives from the health and social services and the voluntary sector) and on joint care planning teams which are offshoots of the former. Public meetings can be held to give them the opportunity to state their views and to affirm that their opinions are valued. At an informal level, discussions can be held with carers' groups or with individual carers. Questionnaires and surveys can be used to canvass their opinions, as can the local press and radio.

The voluntary sector, particularly the co-ordinating bodies such as Councils of Voluntary Service, can be very important in encouraging consultation with carers. They are frequently the voluntary sector representatives on the relevant consultative committees and can therefore ensure that the carers' viewpoint is expressed. In addition they, or individuals connected with them, can act as advocates on behalf of carers. This advocacy role is quite well established as far as disablement groups go — the voluntary sector has been very successful in either promoting the cause of disabled people or, more satisfactorily, helping disabled people themselves to promote it. The time is right for them to play a similar role with carers, and there is evidence that they are beginning to do so, in collaboration with carers' organisations.

Of course, it is one thing to state that you are committed to providing opportunities for carers to participate in consultation, and quite another to ensure that they actually do so. Carers are often quite unused to being members of formal committees or having any opportunities to express their views. It is easy for the power imbalance to be so great that the carers feel quite unable to speak. Formal committee procedures are daunting and inhibiting to many lay people: carers may need training in how to cope or, better still, committees should be prepared to make their proceedings easier to understand and less daunting. A special item on the agenda about carers, or response to points made by them, may help. It should be made clear to the carer in what capacity he or she is participating, whether as an individual or as a representative of a group, and other committee members should accept that it may be necessary for the carer to speak about her own experiences and that she may need time for this.

Finally, a few important points about making the consulting of carers a reality, not a token gesture. They should be involved at the **beginning**, at the earliest stages of planning. So-called 'retrospective' consultation, after a policy has been decided, or to validate it when it is no longer possible to change it, is no use to anyone. Carers are very busy people and they need the assurance that the time they spend, often at the expense of having to get someone in to care for the dependent person, is of some significance. The purpose of the consultation must be made clear and its results must be communicated to the carer.

Incidentally, the carers' dimension should not be limited to obvious things like planning respite care services. Carers no doubt have opinions about how disabled access to parks and gardens or leisure areas affects them, how transport is provided and whether or not educational services are accessible to them, as well as many other things. Only when we are able to provide satisfactory answers to the question, 'What is the carer angle on this?' to the whole range of service provision and policy-making, will we truly be able to say that carers are adequately recognised.

RESPITE

They offered to find someone to sit with him every Thursday

*afternoon, but what I really needed was a night's sleep, or (what a
blissful thought) two nights' sleep.*

In Chapter 6 I said that in order to be effective and really
valuable to carers, respite care must be accessible, it must
be flexible and it must be appropriate to their circumstances. Let us now examine in more detail the sort of
principles which should be borne in mind by policy-makers
and service deliverers when planning respite care.

First, because there is a wide variety of need, there must
be a wide variety of provision. A range of options should be
available to carers to reflect their different needs and the
different needs of the people for whom they are caring.
Some families may need frequent short breaks, others a
longer break once or twice a year. Some want respite care
which is provided in the home, others want the cared-for
person to be admitted to a home or hospital, still others
want a mixture of both. All types should be available, and
all Local Authorities and health authorities should adopt a
'mixed economy' principle in organising respite care. They
should bear in mind, too, that for the carer, time for themselves should not always mean that they should have to
leave the house. Carers frequently say that what they
would like would be to have the house to themselves for an
afternoon, so that taking the dependent person out will
give the carer an important period of quiet and peace. The
value of privacy in one's home is something which it is easy
to forget.

*I am grateful for the people who come in to help when I have to go
to London occasionally, but if a team of four people has to be
organised to cover the whole day, that's four people who can come
in, look in my fridge, use my crockery, answer my phone and so
on. I can't help resenting the lack of privacy sometimes.*

Day care, various fostering schemes and sitting services
should all be available, and to take account of her changing
needs and those of the dependant, the carer should have an
opportunity regularly to review the situation. There is

nothing worse than feeling one has to go on accepting a particular form of respite when it is no longer meeting anyone's needs satisfactorily.

Notice should not necessarily be required to gain access to respite care. Emergencies arise, such as the carer becoming ill or a sudden deterioration in the condition of the cared-for person, and then carers should have immediate access to respite care. Services should never be withdrawn without notice or consultation, and access to them should always be as easy as possible, with the minimum number of bureacratic procedures.

Whenever possible, residential respite care should be provided as near to the normal home as possible, so that the person cared for can be visited and feel in touch with family and friends. Transport systems should be taken into account — how will a family without a car get to the home or hospital? The cost of transport should be considered, too.

Helping carers to use respite care is at least as important as actually providing it. We have seen how guilt on the part of the carer, and reluctance on the part of the person cared for, can mean that the carer does not always feel able to take advantage of what is available. It is therefore necessary, if a service is to be effective, for service providers to be closely in touch with carers, so that they can understand their needs and their relationship with the dependant, and be prepared to act as negotiator to try to resolve any conflict between the carer's need for a break and the dependant's reluctance to accept a change, however temporary. Because of this, it is essential that, as early as possible in the caring process, carers are encouraged to see that good quality respite care is an expected and integral part of caring and fundamental to its long-term success. Respite care which is provided only at times of crisis will compound carers' feelings of guilt at 'not being able to cope', and make them even more reluctant to take advantage of it in future. It is most likely to be effective when properly planned and regularly used from the outset. This may mean that some services and institutions will need to promote their services and include an education element. Some residential units, for example, employ an outreach worker to build links with the community, and to encourage groups to hold evenings and meetings on the premises, so that carers can visit and become familiar with the place.

Simple written information about services is essential in order to inform carers and professionals and ensure appropriate referrals. It should describe the service and its aims, give details of any charges and whom to contact. Care should be taken to ensure that the information is kept up to date and that it is available in appropriate languages if necessary.

Because carers are often reluctant to give the care of 'their' dependant over to anyone whom they don't think can do it as well as they, time should be taken to establish trust, and care staff should have training in the special needs of those in respite care and their carers. Carers should be encouraged to be involved in the planning and management of services — for example, serving on committees or advisory groups.

In summary, carers should be encouraged to understand that they have rights to good quality relief care, and those who provide it should realise that the provision of an effective service depends on them being closely in touch with carers, understanding their needs and the needs of the people they care for.

INFORMATION

Why doesn't anyone tell you anything? More than that, why do they make it so bloody difficult to find anything out?

This sort of statement is heard from almost every carer. Carers need information badly — about the services available in their area, about the benefits to which they are entitled, about being a carer, about changes in legislation which will affect them, and about the condition of the person for whom they are caring. Why is it that so many of them find it so difficult to get *any* of those, let alone all of them?

One explanation is probably connected with recognition of the caring role. Because carers so often do not think of themselves as a 'carer', but only as a 'wife', a 'father' or a 'daughter', they do not connect the specialness of the role with a need for specific information. Another is that caring is of itself an isolating and energy-sapping experience, leaving carers with no contacts who will pass on information and no energy to seek it out. Yet another explanation lies in the fact that it is not the responsibility of any single agency or individual to provide carers with the necessary information, and in consequence it is often a matter of chance whether the carer finds something out or not.

One remedy for this situation is a 'one door' or 'one stop' policy on giving information to carers. Establishing a Carers' Centre can, for example, provide a focal point for all carers' needs, and can co-ordinate all the different sources of information under one roof. These centres have usually been set up by voluntary organisations, assisted by the statutory sector. They generally have at least one full-time worker and can be the focus not only for disseminating information but also for advocacy on behalf of carers, or for specific projects, such as work with ethnic minority carers.

A single-door centre can be very effective, but the only way really to ensure that sufficient information is received by carers is to make every agency and service which comes into contact with them feel responsible for providing information. As long as people think it is someone else's job, they won't do it themselves. It should be mandatory on all those who come into any contact with carers to provide information, or at least to ensure that the carer knows where to get it. There can never be too much encouragement given to carers to seek help, given their extreme reluctance to ask for anything for themselves. Information should always be given as sensitively and simply as possible, since carers are very easily discouraged and haven't the time or inclination to speak to endless different departments or individuals. As they are often unconvinced that they have any right to a service in the first place, they will certainly not have the courage to persist if they are not treated sympathetically and understandingly.

My doctor did say that if I got in touch with the Council they could tell me about someone who helps you with incontinence. So I rang the DHSS but they said it was Social Services. I rang there but it was the wrong division, and then they put me on to someone else but the person I needed wasn't there that day. I've never bothered since because it's so awkward to keep ringing from a call-box. My neighbour says I can use her phone, but it's embarrassing to talk about mother soiling the bed when you can be overheard.

A 'saturation' policy is really necessary when trying to get information over to carers. You have to use not only every professional and voluntary agency with whom they may come into contact, but also make information available in doctors' surgeries, libraries, post offices, launderettes, newsagents — even milkmen. Carers' handbooks, newsletters, fact-sheets and packs are useful. Great care must be taken not to use professional jargon and to present material as accessibly as possible. The design of leaflets and other material is very important, and it is vital that the illustrations reflect the multi-cultural nature of our society. A leaflet about respite care services which contains only pictures of white people will make, say, an Asian carer, feel that the service is not available to her. However good the written material is, many people have difficulty absorbing things which must be read, and here the local radio and television can be extremely effective, as I have described in Chapter 6.

Local carers' groups can of course be absolutely vital in passing on information, and Local Authorities should always ensure that they use them as a communication channel. They should ensure, too, that their personnel have good communication skills and understand that carers are often so distressed that this may act as a barrier to hearing the information.

This is particularly the case when it comes to information about the condition of the dependent person. It is important that professionals and carers understand the position of the carer who wrote to me recently:

As soon as the doctor said it was Alzheimer's Disease, my mind went blank. He told me lots about it and was very kind, but I just couldn't take it in and I just couldn't think what to ask when he said did I have any questions? If only I could have gone back next day and spoken to him when I wasn't so shocked.

This particular carer got in touch with Carers National Association who put her on to the Alzheimer's Disease Society, but many carers never have the opportunity to ask or find out the information they need.

They should know both the prognosis for the disease and how the sufferer can be most effectively cared for. In practice, few receive this information. Medical practitioners often make the judgement that the carers would prefer not to hear bad news. Carers, however, are virtually unanimous in saying that they *do* want to know, because if they do not they only imagine the worst, and that they need as much information as possible in order to provide the best care they can. I suspect that the practice of keeping the information to themselves may be more to do with the medical practitioners saving themselves the distress, than with saving the carers any anxiety.

There may of course be other reasons why a full diagnosis of the condition cannot be given, — for example, the sufferer himself may prefer them not to know. If the doctor or other professional is unable to give a diagnosis or prognosis, either because the sufferer has asked him not to, or simply because he does not know, then carers should be told this and given explanations. They should also be given reasons for all treatment, or changes in treatment, and should have access to a second opinion from any specialist. They should always be encouraged to read the many excellent publications put out by national organisations which are specifically focused on a disease, like Parkinson's, Alzheimer's, or Multiple Sclerosis.

In short, the carers' need for information, both about what they need for themselves and about the nature of the illness if any, should be regarded as positive. It should be regarded as everyone's job to provide them with as much information as possible to help them be more effective and less stressed in their role.

Practical Help

If I'd had to describe my life before I got the hoist for the bath and the incontinence service, I'd have said it was sheer hell. I can't say it's heaven now exactly, but at least it's bearable.

As we have seen, caring for a heavily dependent person involves a huge amount of heavy physical work which is often necessary 24 hours a day. Carers therefore need assistance, both human and mechanical, aids and adaptations to the home, help with transport and incontinence services. Many authorities provide these, but it is essential for policy-makers to accept that these services should be provided for the benefit of carers, to fit in with their particular needs, not at the convenience of the provider, conforming to patterns which suit *them*.

Because much practical help in the home has been developed to suit the needs of frail elderly people living alone, it is often not well suited to the needs of carers. The traditional type of home help service, for example, where the home help came in at the same time each day and did specific household tasks, is not as suitable or valuable for carers as the type of Crossroads Care scheme which is more flexible and adaptable, and which starts from the principle of substituting exactly for the carer. So the tasks *may* be housework or ironing, but may equally well be sitting with the dependent person while the carer goes out shopping. Many Local Authorities are in fact changing their home help services into home care services, which operate more on the care attendant model. Policy-makers may have to face difficult decisions about whether the existing service can be adapted in a way which will make it suitable for carers, or whether they will have to provide something completely new. Flexibility of services can be achieved in other ways, too. Voluntary organisations can be commissioned to provide services of a flexible kind, or various forms of care, such as paid good neighbours, can be bought in.

An innovative and imaginative approach is also necessary when services for carers are being planned. The carer who said, 'What I need is a clone of me to be here when I can't be,' made a telling point. Local Authorities can experiment with this 'clone' idea. They need to provide services which fit in with the way of life already established between the carer and the cared-for person. One carer, for example, had been used to doing a part-time job on Tuesdays and Thursdays while her mother was at the Day Centre. Her employer then needed to change the hours of her particular shift from 11 a.m. to 3 p.m., to 12 noon to 4 p.m. As the Day Centre closed at 3 p.m., the carer thought she would be unable to continue with the job. This distressed her very much as it was a lifeline to her and enabled her not only to earn a little extra money, but also to keep up some social contacts.

She spoke to the social worker about her problem and, instead of just sympathising as the carer had expected, the social worker set about trying to find out whether she could re-organise services to help. She eventually found two neighbours who, if paid a small sum by the Social Services Department, would agree to come to the house, one on Tuesday and one on Thursday, to receive the mother when she came home from the Day Centre, make her a cup of tea and wait with her until the carer came home. The carer was able to continue with her job and keep up the outside contacts which were so important to her.

In this case, as in so many, the amount of paid help necessary was in fact very small, only two hours a week, but the difference it made to the carer's life was immense. A similar flexible approach can provide out of hours help for carers. What do you do if you are alone with a heavy elderly person who falls out of bed at night? Some Local Authorities have paid helpers or good neighbours or street wardens, who can be called on to help in just such an emergency.

Other forms of practical help which should be provided are washing machines or dryers, telephones (46 per cent of elderly people in England have no telephone), and also a wide range of aids and equipment. Walking frames, bath seats, specially designed feeding cups and plates, clothing which fastens with velcro tape rather than with buttons, and a range of specialised equipment for helping to manage incontinence, should all be available to the carer as a matter of course. Not all carers will want to take advantage of these, but they should be given the choice.

As well as simple equipment, adaptations to the home should also be available. A ramp, a handrail, a bath hoist or perhaps a stair lift can make a huge difference to the ease with which someone is cared for. They should be available to carers as soon as practicably possible. At present, alterations to dwellings especially can take a long time to arrange. Although grants from the Local Authority may be available to help with conversions, these too can take a long while to organise and would be greatly helped if a professional, who knows her way about the system, could be available to make the arrangements on the carer's behalf. Where the carer is an owner-occupier there will be no problem about the adaptations at a later date, but where the property is a Council one, carers may have a real problem after the death of the dependent person. For example, is it right that someone should go on living in a Council property which has been specially adapted for a disabled person, when the carer herself is able-bodied and no longer has need of the adaptations? Yet the house or flat is her home: should she be expected to move? The situation must be explained at the outset and negotiations should be sensitively handled.

Two more important points must be made before we leave the subject of practical help. The first is that the carer's needs for practical help should be **regularly reviewed**. Too many carers report that they turned down an offer at an early stage of caring, 'because we didn't need it then', whereas several years later they are now in great need of, say, an incontinence service, but no one has ever asked them about it again. Secondly, practical help must always be offered with real regard to the particular circumstances of the carer. Nowhere is this more necessary, or more often overlooked, than in dealing with the needs of carers from ethnic minorities. A large proportion of elderly carers from this group do not speak English, yet access to welfare benefits, or to the knowledge that services exist, may depend on your ability to read English. Lack of a common language may also mean that carers cannot be taught the practical skills which will make caring easier. Many Local Authorities are proud of the fact that they offer services equally to all sections of the population, but that very point can make them inaccessible to some carers. Meals on wheels services spring to mind: meals are provided, but most of them would be unacceptable to Asian carers and dependants. Certain cultural differences will also mean that no male attendant could help a female person.

To sum up, the quantity and quality of service provided to carers should be constantly reviewed and monitored, and opportunities found for carers to feed back to service providers how far the services are meeting their needs.

MONEY

Somehow I can cope with feeling trapped by having to care for father, but feeling trapped in poverty, that's hard.

Caring costs, as I have said before. The financial effects can be devastating, varying greatly according to the degree of disability of the person being cared for and the length of the caring period. Extra heating, extra washing, special equipment, special food, transport, substitute care, all put a huge strain on household budgets. A cost much less easy to quantify is the loss of income suffered by a carer because he or she is no longer able to work. When we think, therefore, about what should be done for carers as far as money is concerned, we should be prepared to think of helping them to claim the maximum rate of benefit to which they are entitled, and of ensuring that they are enabled to continue working or to take up employment wherever possible.

Maximising Benefits

Until 1975 there was no specific provision at all for people looking after a disabled relative or friend. The introduction of Invalid Care Allowance was a belated response to the financial needs of carers and is completely inadequate, largely because of the restrictions which apply to the receipt of the benefit — it is an income replacement benefit, so is not available to women over 60 or men over 65. Until June 1986 there was a fundamental restriction that ICA could not be received by married or cohabiting women. This was finally removed only after it became evident that the European Court of Justice was about to rule that the exclusion of these women breached an EEC directive on Equal Opportunities (see Chapter 4). Since the rules were changed, it is believed that more than 90,000 women have been awarded ICA. This is believed to be a very low figure compared with the numbers who are entitled to the benefit, but many people do not claim it either because they are reluctant to seek payment for something they do for love, or because they fear, often rightly, that claiming this benefit will result in losing others under the so-called 'overlapping benefits' rule.

All those who come into contact with carers should see it

as part of their job to ask them about their financial situation, to ensure that they know what is available to them and to reassure them that they have a *right* to the money. Our benefits system is a complex one and I am not suggesting that every doctor should become a welfare benefits adviser and every social worker a claimants' advocate. Nonetheless, if the doctor asks the carer if she is getting benefits, it indicates to her that claiming is expected and therefore acceptable; and if the social worker happened to carry claim forms with her when visiting carers and perhaps checked occasionally that they had managed to fill them in correctly, carers would be greatly helped. If this could be accompanied by a local 'take-up' campaign, to raise awareness about what is available, with local radio programmes, leafleting, and articles in the local papers, the take-up rate would be very much increased. Many carers find their local carers' group extremely helpful in this respect: if they speak to other carers who make claims, they not only get practical advice about how to do it but also feel it is 'OK' to do so.

Carers and Work

It is difficult to estimate the costs of caring in terms of loss of income. In 1982, some research indicated that it was likely to be in the region of £89 per week, and that of course does not take into account any estimate of the loss of promotion opportunities which may result from caring.

Wherever possible, carers should be helped to retain their jobs. This is important not only from the point of view of money, but because of the psychological importance the job may have for the carer and the emotional support which can be gained from colleagues in the workplace. Local services should be provided, therefore, in a way which fits in with the carer's needs, and flexible approaches are vital, such as that of the social worker in the case study described above in the section on practical help. The length of the day at a Day Centre — does it really have to close at 3pm?

The hours worked by care attendants — can their shift be made to fit in with shifts at the local factory? These things should be taken into consideration when services are being planned.

Most important of all, those who work with carers should keep an open mind about the desirability of carers continuing with their jobs. Too often, as we have seen in various case studies, carers, especially if they are female, are simply expected to stop working and become carers. Too frequently, help to continue working is given reluctantly if at all, and the carer feels that what she is asking for is in some way unreasonable. If professionals take that attitude, the carer will feel that if she were a *really* loving daughter or wife she would not be thinking about her own need to keep the job, but about the greater need of her husband, parent or child.

Employers, too, have a part to play here. Lack of understanding and sympathy on their part can make it impossible for carers to keep on working. Flexible hours, some kind of carer's leave, understanding attitudes about a sudden crisis — all these are necessary. How many sick days are in actual fact the sickness of the dependant? No amount of good planning can prevent difficulties cropping up in the home situation, which is why flexibility is needed. Perhaps carers could be allowed to make up lost time later, when they can perform better than they do under stress. In many workplaces employers provide flexible arrangements for child care. These should be extended to include arrangements for carers. While flexible hours make it possible for carers to cope with a short crisis, they should also be entitled to unpaid, or perhaps even paid, leave to help them cope with more serious crises. Employers and trades unions should reach a specific agreement to cover the needs of carers for family or compassionate leave. It can be done, because some employers have already reached agreements for up to five or ten days' leave each year to be granted on compassionate grounds to those with caring responsibilities.

Another way in which employers could help would be to encourage the setting up of **workplace support groups** with the help of trades unions. As a first step, a letter could be sent to all staff, inviting those who were carers to attend for an informal meeting. One employee should be given specific responsibility for servicing the group, and the tasks would include arranging for outside speakers, and liaison with the local Social Services Department and the local branches of carers' organisations.

Forging links with the local community is another way in which employers can help carers. Local voluntary and community organisations can be very helpful, for example, in arranging transport or sitting services, and the employer can help carers find out about these services and encourage them to make use of them. Employers could also turn their attention to giving help, either financial or in kind, to these local groups in order to forge better links. Providing help with production of their newsletter, or a grant towards a new piece of office equipment, could help relationships between voluntary organisations and employers, enabling the voluntary organisations to extend their services.

An Income for Carers

We can do what we can to ensure that carers maximise their income, but the major responsibility for income maintenance provision rests with central government, both for those who need care and for those who provide it. Disabled people and those who care for them will continue to be disadvantaged in society and be unable to participate fully as citizens, unless they have a right to an income which covers the costs of disability on the one hand and the costs of caring on the other. The only benefit currently available to informal carers, the Invalid Care Allowance, has very serious shortcomings. For a start, it is too low, at the time of writing only £26.20 per week. Whether you get it or not is dependent on the person you are caring for receiving the Attendance Allowance — in itself a problem. Attendance

Allowance is not paid until six months after the onset of the disability, and is hedged around with so many restrictions that as many as 50 per cent of claims are turned down first time round and have to go to appeal (naturally not every claimant bothers to appeal). Those who receive ICA are only allowed to earn £12 a week before the benefit is affected, and because of the overlapping benefits rule, ICA is not available to anyone over retirement age, or to married women whose spouses are also claiming benefit.

A major review of the benefits system for carers is necessary and this should be coupled with a review of the income for disabled people. It is necessary for the two to be done together since it is important to keep in balance the rights of both groups. It is often suggested that all disablement income should be paid to the disabled person, who could then 'buy in' the services of a carer. This approach does not in my view sufficiently recognise the special nature of the caring relationship. Caring is not a business relationship but an emotional one, and the notion of 'buying in' can cause great upset, as well as there being no guarantee whatsoever that the carer would actually receive the income. The Attendance Allowance itself is intended to 'buy in' care, but in many families it is jealously guarded by the recipient and the carer has to do the buying in out of her own pocket.

There are two aspects to an adequate income for carers. The first is a **carers' pension**. This should be paid to all carers of working age, who are unable to work because of the time they spend looking after someone with a disability. Unlike the current ICA, it should be paid at the rate of other benefits, such as the rate of the retirement income, and the earnings rule should be similarly less restrictive — You are allowed to earn £75 a week on retirement pension. Receipt of the carer's pension should qualify the carer for a full retirement pension and should be paid for six months following the death of the person cared for or his or her entry into full-time residential care, in order to help with a period of re-adjustment.

The second aspect relates to the actual costs of caring and should be called a **carers' allowance**. This should be paid directly to the carer and should be non-means tested, tax free and should be disregarded for the purposes of calculating rights to other benefits. So if you are a carer, you should get it **no matter what other benefits you are receiving**.

In short, in order that carers receive enough money adequately to carry out their caring role, we should ensure that the conditions surrounding the payment of benefits should not trap them into a full-time carer role unless that is what they want; that they should be able to continue with their employment if they so choose; and that there should be as much flexibility as possible in the system to encourage shared care. Choices are important.

* * *

We have looked at what should be done to satisfy the needs of carers for recognition, for respite, for practical help and for money, but there is another need interwoven with all these, and that is the need for continuity of support which is appropriate and which responds to changing circumstances. One important element of this is help with the process of looking at alternatives to caring, or of giving up caring. Caring is an activity which forces people into a 'closed' emotional system. Everyone has a point of tolerance beyond which they cannot go, and beyond which breakdown is the only alternative open to them: breakdown either in the physical sense — the carer breaks her leg — or in the emotional sense, when she has to receive psychiatric treatment. A carer does not work set hours, have any rights to annual leave, usually no entitlement to sick leave, and often no notion at all of when she should stop caring. It is therefore vital that the support and reassurance she receives should continue until she is no longer willing or able to go on caring, and then other alternatives should be available.

Similarly, no carer should ever feel forced to take on the caring role in the first place. Informal care is not always the ideal form of care for every person who needs help. Not everyone who needs care has a relative or friend who wants to do it, and not every potential carer feels able to take it on. Opportunities should always be given to refuse the role of carer: people should never be made to feel, either by implication or suggestion, that it is their duty, nor should lack of alternative forms of care be a deciding factor. Carers should be offered counselling to help them with what they may very well find a difficult decision, and service providers and gatekeepers should be aware of their own attitudes in such a situation. While not saying anything directly, it is common for professionals to put over their own ideas about 'duty' and 'obligation', especially where they hold stereotyped views, as most of us do, about what is the 'right' course of action. A social worker who subscribes to the view that Asian families always look after their own is unlikely to be open and unjudgemental when an Asian family wants to explore the possibility of alternative forms of care.

Even when family care has been provided successfully for many years, the time will probably come when it is no longer the most appropriate choice. Carers then need as much information as possible about available alternatives, opportunities to talk through all the possibilities, perhaps some counselling to help them with the decision, the chance to visit homes and hospitals and talk with staff and residents. It may take them a long while to make up their minds.

No decisions of this kind can be made without the participation of the person cared for: the carer does not have the power to make decisions about other people's lives, any more than the policy-makers or service providers do. How much the disabled person can participate will of course depend on the nature and degree of his or her disability. Someone who is physically disabled will be able to partici-

pate fully, an elderly, mentally confused person, very little.
But it should not automatically be assumed that being cared
for at home is necessarily the ideal solution and that everything else is therefore in some way second best. The role of
the professional as mediator or negotiator will again be of
the utmost importance, as of course will be the adequate
provision of residential care.

Many carers reading this chapter will have the reaction,
'If only':

> If only I was recognised.
> If only I could get some relief.
> If only I had all or even some of those services.
> If only I had enough money.
> If only someone understood.

All carers should have all the things I have said they
need, as of right. As the Director of Social Services quoted
at the beginning of this chapter said, 'They seem to want so
little.' In the next chapter I shall consider the prospects for
the 'if onlys' being turned into reality for all carers.

8   Is it Likely?

I looked after my father for ten years until March this year. Since then I've had a breakdown with the stress of it and trying to see my way forward after he was gone. Caring for him is an experience which will stay with me for ever. My doctor has been very good but now I'm on my own, it's like a bomb has made a crater and I am trying to make sense of the future. It's too late for me but I hope others can be helped.

Can others be helped? As I have said, it is not difficult to get policy-makers, service providers, researchers, academics, government spokespersons and carers themselves to agree on what should be done for carers. Two questions therefore present themselves: Why does it not happen? Is it likely to happen in the future?

What Prevents Recognition of Carers?

I believe that the key to this lies in the conflicts and dilemmas which seem to be inherent and perhaps unsolvable when we consider the position of carers. Let us look at those conflicts and examine them from three points of view: those of the individuals concerned, the service deliverers and professionals, and society as a whole.

The Individual

As I said in Chapter 4, the workhouse was officially abolished in 1948, but it casts its long shadow over our social attitudes still; the idea that it is better to be cared for in one's own home rather than go into an institution is very deeply embedded in our individual consciousnesses, and indeed in the consciousness of the nation. Few people would argue that a person needing care would usually prefer to be looked after at home, at least given the present availability of suitable and acceptable alternative care. These feelings do not seem to be an inevitable part of the human condition, since in many other countries, notably the United States, the expectation of spending at least a part of one's life in some kind of institutional care seems to be accepted. In the United Kingdom, however, the feeling persists that those who are cared for in any kind of institution are in some way failures — perhaps in the material sense because they cannot afford a better form of care, perhaps emotionally because the implication is that no one loves them; or perhaps physically and psychologically because they are 'too bad' to be cared for at home.

But can this form of home care, which is thought to be so desirable, only be given **at the expense of carers**? Must the price inevitably be that carers lead a restricted life? At the very least, the two elements are inextricably entwined and it is impossible to look at the needs of the carer without considering those of the dependent person.

The conflicts which the person being cared for may experience are very great — for some at least, a desire for independence and a fear of being a burden contrast with the feeling that they have the right to be cared for in a way which is acceptable to them, and the right to be helped to maintain as normal a life as possible. The conflicts for carers are even greater. They may perhaps have to weigh the love and duty they feel for one family member with the love and duty they feel for another. Often they must weigh their own desire and right to a career they enjoy, or a job they very much need, with the guilt they feel if they even consider not taking on the carer role. The inevitable conflict between their own needs and those of someone else may lead them to a breakdown, either physical or mental, particularly if they suffer the added stress of finding that the reality of caring is very different from their imaginings.

Caring takes place within the context of a relationship, which may be good or bad, fulfilling or unfulfilling, a fantasy or a reality. The caring relationship has many similarities with others — for example, people have unrealistic expectations of it, and it is a two-way street — but in many important ways it is unlike any other. With most relationships, all parties to it usually enjoy some kind of reciprocity — I'll help you today and you'll help me tomorrow; and some kind of negotiation rights — if you behave in that way, it's not acceptable to me, so can you change that aspect of your behaviour? There is very little negotiation within the caring relationship. This may be because the cared-for person is not easy to negotiate with, owing to some impairment in the faculties such as senile dementia, for example; or it may be because the carer in some sense gave up her negotiation rights at an earlier stage in the relationship, usually in the interests of a 'quiet life'.

Another way in which the caring relationship is not typical is that there are certain emotions it does not permit. A carer is not allowed to be angry with the cared-for person, not allowed to resent the effect he or she is having on her life. The son who has to miss school to come home to take his mother to the lavatory, and to change her when she menstruates, may be praised by everyone for being such a caring child, but he is not permitted to feel angry with his mother for 'causing' his situation. This, of course, does not stop him feeling angry, it just means he has no way of legitimising his anger — a common predicament for carers.

In theory, the biggest conflict should be the choice about whether to care at all. I say 'in theory' because, in my experience, the conflict is more potential than actual. Few carers in practice seem to make that choice. For most there seems to be no question that they should do so — either because of love or because of duty or because of some complicated combination of both. It creeps up on them gradually, so that they are in the situation long before they realise its implications, and certainly too late to retreat from it.

Professionals

Let us look now at the conflicts and dilemmas which confront professionals and which may get in the way of making things better for carers.

I am including a very wide variety of people when I use that word — all those who are called 'carers' as opposed to 'informal carers', for example, those who act as gatekeepers, those who deliver services, those who are involved with carers' organisations at both local and national level. Why is it that, in spite of the very good intentions of most of them, the majority of carers probably still receive no help whatsoever? It is easy enough to get professionals to arrive at a set of agreed principles by which carers should be helped, but putting them into practice requires a fundamental change in the nature of the relationship between the two groups — it requires a shift away from the role of the professional as provider and the carer as recipient.

In many ways the first step in this process has been taken. Carers have been acknowledged as a separate client group with needs of their own, which are different from, though closely linked with, the needs of the dependent person. But there are many professionals who still see carers only in that role of recipient, and who have made no move at all towards seeing the carer as a partner. When I was speaking at a meeting in Scotland recently, a nurse in the audience shared her anxieties about not being able to meet the needs of carers when they asked her for something.

I just feel so terrible that I can't help, and so guilty because of all the carer is having to do, that I know sometimes I rush out of the house instead of staying to talk.

One of the carers who was in the audience responded to her:

But why should you assume I want you to provide me with something? I read the papers. I know about the cuts. What is important is that I know that you understand my position.

Locked in to her own expectation of her role, the nurse was in danger of missing what the carer really wanted from her.

Too many professionals still only ask carers the questions which they know they can answer, rather than questions which may have no answer but which nonetheless should be asked.

Nor is the problem all on the professionals' side. Carers may contribute to it because they, too, have set ideas in the way they view professionals, and may only see them as people who can do something for them. That is not what partnership means: it means that all contributors are of equal value or valued for their own particular contribution. Clearly, there is a problem about gaining this kind of acceptance from professionals who have been trained in certain ways, or who in the course of their work have developed ways of thinking which lock them into the provider role, but the problems and conflicts do not only lie with them.

Undoubtedly, there are problems created by the fact that professionals and carers have quite different things to offer to the caring situation. Professionals are trained in particular skills and have specialised information about a general range of issues. Carers base the work they do on personal knowledge, both of their relationship and of the condition of the person for whom they are caring. For carers, it is very important to distinguish between the role of informal carer, which is part of a relationship and therefore based on some kind of sharing and love, and formal care, which is part of a quite different set of relationships. We have rights to informal care because of love or some notion of duty, whereas we have rights to the formal care offered by professionals as ratepayers, voters or citizens, or to private care as purchasers.

Carers feel special pride in the nature of the caring re-lationship, in the way it takes account of the specific per-sonal needs of the cared-for person. Many even resist the use of the word 'carer' and say fiercely, 'I'm not a carer, I'm a wife, a daughter, a father.' Many are convinced, no doubt quite rightly, that no one can care for the dependent person as well as they: one of the reasons why care attendant schemes are so appreciated is that they replicate, but do not change, the role of carer. Carers want recognition, support, respite, practical assistance and advice, but they want it given within the context of the special relationship between carer and cared-for person. They want (and why shouldn't they?) the support and services offered to respect the nature of that relationship. This poses great problems for services which may have been tailored originally to the needs of disabled people or of people living alone. It may be that adaptation of existing services will not be enough to make them suitable for carers — the service providers may have to start again from scratch.

That brings us to the question of resources. For many professionals, the greatest conflict they have is that there is simply not enough money, and that providing services to carers will mean withdrawing them from some other group. This is an unresolvable dilemma, but the time has certainly come to attempt to even up the balance. For too long scarce resources have been targeted at those who live alone. We should remember that providing support for carers makes sound economic sense. As the Griffiths report on Community Care said, 'A failure to give proper levels of support to informal carers not only reduces their own qual-ity of life and that of the relative or friend they care for, but it is also potentially inefficient as it can lead to less personally appropriate care being offered.'

It is too easy for service deliverers to say that they *would* do it all if only they had the resources. True, more resources are needed, but changes of attitude on the part of both professionals and carers are equally important: all too often, it is the attitudes which stop improvements being made.

These conflicts do not just apply to professionals and service deliverers in the statutory sector, but to voluntary organisations too, especially those which work with carers. Some people have commented on the so-called 'professionalisation' of the carers' movement, arguing that the amount of research generated in recent years has provided jobs for professional workers of all kinds, with little or no impact on the quality of life of the average carer. This move towards a professional carers' movement led to much heart-searching among the members who worked so hard to bring about the merger of the Association of Carers with the National Council for Carers and their Elderly Dependants, into the Carers National Association. If we wished to speak with a stronger voice for carers, we had to become a stronger organisation — that was the reason for embarking on a merger in the first place. That meant we had to have more members. More members meant better systems and more work, therefore we had to have adequate staff to deal with them. Therefore we had to increase our funding and use our funds effectively. In order to do so, we had to set up proper monitoring systems and make uncomfortable choices about what services we could and could not provide. We went to infinite pains to ensure not only that the voice of the carer would be heard within the new organisation, but that carers would actually hold power and develop the policy within it. Even so, we are not immune from the sort of criticism to which all so-called consumer-based organisations are vulnerable. It can always be said that the only kind of consumer who is really able to participate is one who is articulate and confident and sufficiently free of caring responsibilities to be able to attend meetings, or well off enough to be able to buy in substitute care. Therefore, by definition, that carer is not typical of the over-burdened, oppressed, inarticulate carers who actually form the bulk of our membership. Alternatively, people will say that if you train consumers or carers to participate on equal terms with professionals, and be effective committee members or representatives, or indeed, if you pay them to come to meetings so that they can afford to buy substitute care, then again, by definition, they are no longer typical of the group and therefore cannot speak on its behalf.

Society

I turn now to the conflicts which are inherent for society itself in recognising the role of informal carers.

I have spoken several times about the desirability of carers having choices. That, of course, should not just mean choice between services but also a choice about whether to care or not to care. *What would we, as a society, do if all carers decided to stop caring, or even if many more of them started to exercise their right to refuse?* There are several demographic changes taking place which would support the view that this is likely to start happening more and more in the near future.

The availability of women carers is one such change, and we have seen that women make up by far the majority of the caring population. On average, a couple married in 1920 would have had, by the age of 80, 42 female relatives of whom 14 would not be working. A couple born in 1925 and married in 1950 will, when they reach the age of 75 in 2000, have an estimated 11 female relatives of whom only three will not be working.

Not only are there fewer women, but more of them are working. In 1985 a Labour Force Survey revealed that three quarters of women aged 35 to 49, and three fifths of those aged 50 to 59, were in paid work, although half of those were part-time workers. The pool of informal carers is thus substantially reduced.

The increased mobility of the population is a factor, too. The increase in short-distance migration from one part of the country to another, whether in search of work, promotion or a change of scene, means that the tightly-knit, locally based, working class neighbourhoods described in the sociological studies of the 1950s are increasingly a thing of the past. We are living in a more fragmented society, one in which people are more home-centred, watching their videos and playing with their home computers, rather than looking outwards into the community in which they live.

Another factor might be that a new generation of potential carers is growing up — a generation much more used to asking, even demanding, their rights. They have grown up with the idea that it is the State's duty to provide for those who are not able to provide for themselves, and they may be considerably more vocal in asking for what they want, or more resolute in refusing to change their lives to accommodate caring, than their mothers were.

When I speak to professional groups, especially doctors, I often ask them, 'Should all carers have the right to refuse to care?' Their response is almost always the same. They start by nodding their heads vigorously and reassuring me that they would never put pressure on any family member. (Since I frequently speak to carers who *have* had this pressure brought to bear on them, I find it very odd that none of *those* doctors are ever in my audience!) I then say, 'OK. What are you going to do when most of them start saying NO?' I begin to see looks of panic come over their faces at the thought of their surgeries being overrun with sick and disabled people who no longer have carers; at the thought of the blocked beds in geriatric and acute hospitals; and at the idea of social services departments completely overwhelmed! Then they begin to shift a little in their seats and start to use phrases like: 'Well, of course, it is their job to look after their families, really', 'The state just couldn't cope if they didn't', and, 'If they won't do it, who will?'

I do not find it difficult to reassure those doctors that I don't think this wholesale refusal is about to start happening — far from it. Although many carers are angry and resentful, the vast majority *do* seem to regard caring as their duty — a duty they want to go on performing. Why is this so?

Once again, I believe the key lies in conflicts — this time in the way women's role in society is viewed. I am not trying to ignore the role of male carers, but we must acknowledge the fact that the majority of carers are women, and that research has consistently shown that they carry heavier burdens, with less help than male carers receive.

Women's Role

Why is it that many, indeed perhaps most, women still feel that it is their duty to take on the caring role, or are troubled by feelings of guilt if they do not?

It must surely be because, in spite of the great progress towards equality of the sexes which has been made in society in recent years, we still have very stereotyped views of the roles men and women should play. In spite of the fact that most women work outside the home, research repeatedly shows that they continue to carry most of the responsibility for housework and shopping and all the other household tasks, as well as the major responsibility for child care. We are growing more accustomed to, and more tolerant of, women saying they must leave a meeting in order to fetch the children from school, but to hear a man say it is still exceptional. There are, of course, male single parents who bring up the children alone. Think of one you know and recall how often you have heard someone speak admiringly of his prowess in the kitchen or of his faithful attendance at parents' evenings. Do you hear people speak in the same way of single mothers? Of course not — because women are expected to be able to do those things well, whereas people find it notable in a man.

The boy child is spoken of approvingly as 'a real lad', and even the most liberated mother may grow a little anxious if her son plays with dolls too often or keeps saying he wants to be a nurse rather than a doctor. Girls, on the other hand, are expected to be carers from the time they are given the first doll. To be a caring person is a woman's currency in society: she is judged by her 'caringness' as a man is judged by his achievements, or by the extent of his ambition. Similarly, to be seen as uncaring damages a woman's status far more than it does a man's. The words 'tough', 'single-minded', 'ambitious', are terms of admiration or respect when applied to a man, terms of criticism when applied to a woman. A woman's social identity, the way she is perceived by those with whom she comes in contact, is likely to be based on her caring qualities, whereas a man's is more likely to be founded on his achievements. Naturally, this has an effect on the way a woman judges herself. Her own self-esteem is likely to be based on how caring she feels she is, and she may judge herself very harshly if she thinks she lacks caring qualities. Therefore if a woman's ability to be caring is part not only of her own self-esteem, but of the esteem in which she is held by the people around her, it is very difficult for her to refuse to take on the caring role, since in doing so she is downgrading herself, in her own as well as society's eyes.

The second reason why women's role as carers does not seem destined to change radically in the immediate future concerns attitudes to work. Although it is estimated that 75 per cent of women now work outside the home, much of the work they do is part-time. In spite of a divorce rate of one in three marriages, society still seems basically to be organised around the principle that people live in families where there is a male breadwinner and that the woman is dependent on him. As a consequence, women's work is not seen as being of equal importance with that of men. It is supposedly easier for them to give up their jobs, therefore more of them are available for caring. It is surely significant that the only males who seem actually to be *expected* to become carers are those who have retired. Only if they are no longer working are they seen as able to care for their spouses.

Another reason why women may feel they cannot refuse to become or to continue to be carers is, of course, the lack of acceptable alternative forms of care. Faced with what is available in some areas, women may have no option but to feel what society so clearly *expects* them to feel — that care at home is best.

There are great conflicts in this situation for those of us who are working with carers and are actively involved in trying to get a better deal for them in terms of improved services and more financial support. We must ask ourselves: does the provision of better services actually reinforce women's position as men's dependants, with no free choice about how they spend their lives? Do these services provide just enough respite, so that women do not crack up but are enabled to continue coping? If we work for adequate financial rewards for carers, is that, too, reinforcing women's second-class position in the labour market, since it is unlikely that a carer's income is ever going to compare favourably with that of other kinds of employment?

If these things *are* the case, what can we do about it?

I am not suggesting that there is necessarily a solution to these conflicts, but would point out that they influence greatly the way carers are regarded.

It may be that there is nothing we can do but wait for gradual changes in society's expectations of women to take place. Coupled with other changes which we can expect, and which I shall refer to later on, it may be that society's expectations of women as carers *is* changing, slowly, but very surely.

Is better Recognition of Carers likely?

We have seen that there are conflicts in the way carers are viewed by individuals, by professionals and by society. Inevitably we must also look to see whether there are conflicts in the way they are viewed by government, because in the last analysis, real changes in the lives of carers depend on legislation — either legislation which leads and forms public opinion, or legislation which follows the growth of a movement or a groundswell of opinion.

As far as this goes, I have to say that there is good news and bad news. The good news is, as we have seen, that the word carer has appeared in legislation for the first time, in the Disabled Persons Act 1986. There has been a carers' debate in Parliament and the DHSS has backed a programme of helping the community to care, which has resulted in some splendid projects in three areas of the country and no doubt will provide ideas and valuable experience for others in the future. Carers' organisations are funded by the government, though not generously. Before the 1986 General Election, three of the political parties mentioned carers in their manifestos and government ministers are on record as frequently acknowledging the so-called 'invaluable contribution' of informal carers. Much research has been spawned about carers and we are now more aware of their problems. Moreover, a question in the 1985 Census began to give us more idea about the most basic fact which has so far been lacking — namely, an idea of just how many carers there are. Quite a lot of good news there.

Sadly, though, we must set against this some bad news. A series of government measures seems designed to make life more difficult for carers and to go against its own stated policies — that it is committed to helping and supporting carers. The first of these is the change in social security benefits brought about by the Social Security Act, which came into force in April 1988.

Social Security Act

Some carers benefited from the fact that they are now allowed to have £6,000 capital instead of £3,000, as formerly, before they lose their right to means-tested benefits; moreover, they no longer have to show that giving up their job was the only means by which a disabled person could be cared for, as they had to do under the previous supplementary benefit regulations.

However, these benefits have been outweighed by the

losses. In the Act there is provision for special 'client group' premiums. If you are mentally ill or physically disabled, for example, this will entitle you to an extra payment. There is no extra payment for being a carer. Under the previous supplementary benefit rules, carers could qualify after a certain period for a higher long-term rate of premium. This no longer applies.

Another problem which the Act has caused concerns the particular difficulties carers may have in the early stages. The disabled or dependent person may not claim Attendance Allowance until he or she has been ill for six months. The carer, though not eligible for Invalid Care Allowance until the Attendance Allowance was being paid, used to be able to claim exemption from work availability so that she could claim unemployment benefit. This is no longer possible, and she risks losing her benefit under the increasingly stringent 'availability for work' tests now applied to those who claim unemployment benefits. This problem will be made even worse for carers at the end of the caring period. The insurance credits, which they receive if they get Invalid Care Allowance, used to entitle them to unemployment benefit after the person they were caring for had died or gone permanently into residential care. These credits no longer count in the new tests of recent employment and contribution payments. This part of the Act, which is estimated to prevent about 11,000 carers per year from receiving benefit, was fiercely contested in the House of Commons but to no avail.

Nor is any protection offered to the carer after the caring period has ended, because both those in private rented accommodation and those living in an owned property are under threat. The new Housing Act threatens to take away the right of a carer to succeed to the tenancy of a privately rented house or flat unless she has lived there for two years. This means that, say, a daughter could move in with her mother for almost two years, look after her throughout that time and, when the mother dies, be evicted because she cannot take over the tenancy.

Where a house is owned, the position is very clear under the Social Security Act: disabled or elderly people who are considered to have entered private residential care on a permanent basis will no longer receive income support because they are considered to have a notional capital or over £8,000 in the form of their house. The choice facing the carer who is still living in the house is therefore a stark one. Either she resumes caring for her relative herself, or she must sell the house, or raise a mortgage on it to pay the care home fees. Although this rule does not apply to spouses, only to other relatives, it will effectively make many carers homeless. One remedy is to ensure that the house is transferred to the carer's name before the person cared for is in need of residential care, something which many families find it difficult to discuss, let alone do. Moreover, the potential problems and conflicts within families are very great where there are siblings who are hoping for their share of the value of the house after the death of the dependant.

'Granny' Fostering Schemes

These schemes, which I referred to in Chapter 2, have also suffered under the provisions of the Act. The schemes involve the placement of old people in private homes where they are looked after as a member of the family. Until 1987, old people who had insufficient funds could claim the same rate of benefit as if they were living in a residential home: £130 per week. But, alarmed by reports that an unscrupulous landlord might exploit the scheme and not staff his home properly, legislation was introduced to ensure that two carers must be present in the home, although the two could be husband and wife. Under the Social Security Act, however, a spouse cannot be named as a second carer unless he or she is devoting at least 35 hours a week to the task and has no other employment. Present residents are protected, but when they die and the fostering families seek new residents, they will find that they now qualify, not for £130 a week, but only the ordinary board and lodging rate which, with its elderly supplement, comes to only £67.50 per week.

Abolition of the Dependent Relative's Tax Allowance

At an early stage of its history, the National Council for Carers campaigned for and got acknowledgement of the costs of dependancy in our taxation system. These were the housekeeper's allowance, the son's and daughter's services allowance and the dependent relative's tax allowance. These were summarily wiped out in the April 1988 budget. The Chancellor said that he was taking the opportunity 'to simplify the system' by abolishing three minor personal allowances which had been unchanged in cash terms for over twenty years. It is true that the allowances were small — the dependent relative's allowance was worth only £75 a year — but its abolition meant that one and a quarter million tax payers lost benefit. The Chancellor seemed to feel that because he had been generous in the realms of basic tax, carers ought to appreciate their good fortune and be content. He failed to appreciate that every tax payer would benefit from the improved rates of basic tax and allowances, whereas only carers would suffer from the abolition of the three 'minor' allowances.

The Community Charge (Poll Tax) and Carers

The reform of the rating system, which has taken place in Scotland and will shortly take place in England and Wales, will hit carers hard. For the first time a tax will be payable across the board, irrespective of the individual's income, or his or her ability to pay.

All adults, not only carers themselves but also those they are caring for, must pay at least twenty per cent of the poll tax bill. If carers choose to look after their relatives, they will have to pay the tax for doing so. When families are looking at the best form of care for an elderly or disabled relative they may be forced to consider that if they take that person into their home, they will have to pay the poll tax, whereas if the relative went into residential care, he or she would be exempt. A rebate system is proposed for one group, 'severely mentally handicapped persons', and this is defined as ... 'those who fail to develop normally in childhood'; but thus far there are no exemptions proposed for any other group.

Even if exemptions are introduced, it is likely that the inevitable bureaucracy surrounding them will deter carers from claiming them. Moreover, other difficulties arise when the matter of exemptions is raised, such as proving whether or not a person should be exempted and who should do the exempting. When this was being discussed in the Standing Committee, one MP pointed out that 'Those who have devoted their lives to caring for mentally handicapped people are being expected to suffer the indignity of asking general practitioners to certify them as severely mentally handicapped so that they may be exempted from the poll tax.'

Not only the informal carers themselves will suffer from the introduction of the poll tax, but also those who are closely involved in providing services to them. Many volunteer projects, which rely upon people giving up time to care for others, often for little or no payment, will also be affected.

Paid carers, too, may be worse off. Many of those who work most closely with carers — nurses, care attendants and the like — are among the worst paid members of society. Not only qualified nurses but student nurses too, will be obliged to pay the full poll tax, although other students will only be required to pay 20 per cent. Care assistants who live in residence have been exempt from paying rates but will have to pay the poll tax.

Clearly, the poll tax will have an effect on all forms of caring. Its catch-all nature, irrespective of people's ability to pay or of their circumstances, will bring new burdens to many already hard-pressed groups. Many carers will be placed in the unenviable position of being taxed to care for their own relatives. This seems to run entirely counter to the professed commitment to policies of caring in the community and supporting informal carers. It seems to make the idea of partnerships between formal and informal care, or moving between home care and institutional care, of giving carers adequate respite, even more difficult. How will the amount of poll tax owing be calculated for an old person who spends two nights a fortnight in residential care, two weeks a year being fostered by another family, and who was unexpectedly admitted to hospital for three weeks following a fall?

REALITY VERSUS RHETORIC?

You cannot fail to notice the stark contrast between the rhetoric of official commitments to Community Care and the reality of this series of government policies which seem to run entirely counter to it. The government explicitly relies on informal carers to sustain care in the community policies. As the Griffiths report said, we should *'build first on the available contribution of informal carers'*. Yet at the same time changes are being introduced which will further impoverish and disadvantage carers.

It seems that the needs of carers as a group mirror what happens in the actual caring situation. The carer subordinates her needs to those of the cared-for person. Carers' needs are overlooked because the government pursues other policy goals. Benefits are targeted on other, more visible groups, who are thought to be deserving. We have looked at some of the reasons why this happens — the conflicts inherent in the relationship of carers with other groups in society, the fact that carers are not an easily identifiable group. We have seen that there is little evidence which can be drawn from recent government action of any fundamental change in attitudes to carers. We have seen also, however, that in some ways there is evidence of real changes in the way carers are regarded. We have seen schemes which help them, ways of involving them in planning, and that the growth of a carers' movement has been very influential. What we need to ask now is whether developments are likely in the future which will mean that government policies would be forced to recognise carers more than they appear to do at present.

FUTURE DEVELOPMENTS?

Although the women's movement has thus far had little influence on caring, it is surely inevitable that it will do so in future. So far only a minority of women work at jobs which are truly felt to be on a level with those of men; but that number is increasing and many more women in future will be in jobs which they will not be prepared to abandon to care for a relative. There is also growing up a generation of women who, unlike their mothers, have been used to making child care arrangements which fit in with their working lives. And it is now no longer automatically assumed that a woman who has a baby will give up her job to care for it full time. There is much more expectation that she will consider a range of options for the care of the child. She may consider a full-time child minder, a live-in helper, or part-time work with domestic back-up, her husband or partner may care for the child, or she may choose any combination of those options. In the same way, it is entirely logical that the range of options for caring for an elderly or disabled relative will be considered, too. Mothers who work when their children are babies may still have feelings of guilt, but they are nothing like as bad as those suffered by mothers of an earlier generation. The more people do something, the more acceptable it becomes.

Even if young women did not choose to take this course, it is likely that many of them may be forced into it, since the rate of divorce and the fact that most maintenance payments are never actually received in full will mean that they have no option but to continue with their work. The divorce rate has another effect, too, in that it lessens and weakens the family ties and obligations which lead to caring. You may feel obliged to care for your own mother, but what about your ex-mother-in-law, your step-father or your step-child? Serial monogamy, where people have several marriages in the course of their lives, inevitably leads to people having more relatives, but it is likely that they feel less obligated to provide care for them.

Divorce is one factor in the increasing mobility of the population which is likely to affect patterns of caring. Until comparatively recently, moving from one part of the country to another was an experience confined to the middle classes, but in recent years the search for scarce employment, and especially the imbalance between parts of the country in the amount of work available, have led to many more families being split up and less available to care for each other. Indeed, research shows that we are all likely to become more home based in our activities, with less and less movement outside our immediate family.

Changes in the attitudes of women are likely to affect the caring situation, but so are changes in the situation of those cared for. Elderly people are by far the largest group requiring some form of residential care, and they are commonly seen as an increasing burden because there are more of them, they are living longer and making an increasing demand on services and on carers. It is, however, becoming clearer that some of the common diseases of old age may not necessarily be associated with old age at all, but are rather caused by smoking, unhealthy diet, poor living conditions, or stress, all of which can be changed. If people ate less fat, smoked less and took more exercise, as increasingly they are doing, many of the diseases which have been seen to be an inevitable consequence of old age could be eradicated. Even the hip fractures in elderly women, which are such a frequent cause of prolonged disablement, are now thought to be preventable by prescribing hormone replacement therapy at the menopause, thus preventing the bonewasting disease of osteoporosis. The proportion of the population over pensionable age will remain roughly constant for the next 20 years, at the level of 15 per cent. At the beginning of the next century it will begin to rise again, until it reaches 20 per cent in 2025, but only a minority of these people are likely to require care because of the increased healthiness of the population.

Another important factor to be considered in the future need of the elderly for care is their growing prosperity. In 1985 nearly half of all heads of households aged over 65 were home-owners, and of the next generation, nearly two thirds own their own homes. This, coupled with the fact that many more old people will have occupational pensions — indeed, many couples will have two occupational pensions — will mean that old people requiring care will be considerably better off and that caring is far less likely to be so hedged around with poverty as it is at present. There will, of course, still be a discrepancy between those who own houses in the prosperous South-East and those who own them in the north of England, but the wealth which a house provides will in turn provide both carers and cared-for people with more choice than hitherto about the ways in which care is arranged.

It may be, too, that the way in which we regard residential care will change in future. When the Wagner committee reported, early in 1988, it was clear that many people liked living in old people's homes. Many wrote in to the committee, praising their homes and describing in the most affectionate terms the 'loving family atmosphere' they enjoyed. The Wagner committee chose the title 'A Positive Choice' for the report, as an indication that they wanted to 'promote a fundamental change in the public perception' of residential homes as places into which elderly people would *choose* to go at the latter stages of their lives. If this change does take place, it will, coupled with the gradual fading away of the spectre of the workhouse, mean that far more people requiring care might be prepared to look for it elsewhere than their families.

The Wagner report recommends, for example, that living in a residential establishment should be a positive experience which ensures a better quality of life than could be enjoyed in any other setting. Residents should retain their rights as citizens, and those rights should be safeguarded. They should have access to leisure facilities and educational opportunities, and should be able to receive relatives and friends as they choose. The standards in the home should be those of the best of those currently operating — no one should have to share a room, for example; everyone should be able to lock their own room and to handle their own money. If these standards were the accepted norm for residential homes, not only would many more elderly people choose to live in them, but carers too would be more willing to encourage their elderly relatives to live there.

It is possible that even more radical approaches will gain in popularity. Our present criterion for providing social care is based very much on the family model. In the field of child care we favour adoption and foster homes, for elderly people we favour domiciliary services. The nuclear family, with the man as breadwinner and the woman as carer, is the standard by which we base our ideal forms of care — never mind the reality that very few families are actually like that. By contrast, a collectivist approach would see all citizens as the responsibility of the rest of society. Those performing caring roles and those in need of care would be part of a network of reciprocal relationships, based not on the family but on the whole of society. With this approach, care work would be valued equally with other forms of work, and those delivering it, whether family or professional carers, would be paid accordingly. Instead of trying to provide forms of care which imitate family life, we would be valuing caring in its own right. Thus an old people's home would be valued for the opportunity it gives the elderly people to share the experience of living together, not as a second best to family care.

It may be, then, that the picture is not all gloom for the

future and that there are hopeful signs on the horizon. Perhaps in years to come we shall look back in wonder at the burdens which were once placed on carers, in the same way that we now look back in amazement at a society which once allowed children to work 16 hours a day in a factory. But that day is still a long way off, and even when it comes there will still be a group of people who will not own a house or have access to money, and family members who do not want the house sold to pay for care because they are hoping for their inheritance. And there will still be those, though perhaps fewer of them, who refuse to enter residential care and continue to expect their families to do the caring. Naturally there will also be carers who, given endless choices, will still opt for taking on the task. For these people there can be no lessening of our efforts to improve things for carers. Nor should we confine our efforts to trying to help them cope only. In the research we have done on carers, we may have put too much emphasis on measuring their anxiety and depression, and too much emphasis in our social policy on providing them with services which enable them to cope. Even those who adjust to loss of employment, poverty, social isolation and disrupted family life are nonetheless deprived. Perhaps we should be measuring the quality of life among carers, not just assessing whether or not they are on the verge of a breakdown.

Finally, there is the problem of what happens to carers themselves when they find themselves in need of care. It may be that some have an expectation of reciprocity — that if they care for their mother, their children will in turn care for them — but by and large this does not seem to be the case. They say that they will never do to someone else what was done to them: 'I've told my kids to shoot me when I'm old,' they say. But even if they do not feel like that when the time comes, the caring itself may be preventing them from building up the kind of networks which enable care to take place. They will be isolated from their friends, their families and their local communities. Many will have no opportunity to build up any financial reserves. Who will care for them?

*   *   *

Let the last word be with a carer, to remind us of the urgency of the need.

I am a carer for my husband who is 74 years old. I am 64. My husband has had two strokes and has Parkinson's Disease and arthritis. I am lucky, as he can still hold a general conversation. He can only walk a few feet before he becomes tired and exhausted. He has a battery operated bike which he can operate with his right hand as the second stroke left his left arm paralysed. I have to go with him when he goes on it as he has tunnel vision. I am unable to leave him alone in the house as he is liable to go dizzy and fall, which he very often does. I wash, shave and dress him, help him with his food and I am up during the night with him as he is becoming incontinent. At first I was left in the dark about what help I could get; I had to find my own way. No one advised me at all. It was only through my own determination that I have the help I do have. I have a friend whose daughter-in-law is a district nurse, so I rang her up and she gave me the phone number of the community nurse. Through her I got a bath attendant and a home help, but after so many weeks they said they couldn't come because they was short staffed. But I fought back and I got them back for once a week each. I was given no advice at all and I was given no option as to whether I was capable of looking after my husband or not. It was all taken for granted, and in the process I have come down from nine stone to just over seven stone, which my doctor said was caused by stress. But still no one offers to advise me. I still have to feel my way around. I do not begrudge looking after my husband as I love him very much, but what I do begrudge is the way the system is run as regards carers. You nearly have to go on bended knee for anything you may be entitled to. I don't think I'm being unreasonable when I say that us carers are a forgotten race. Think of all we are saving for the Health Service and the social services by caring for our loved ones at home. You'd think they'd recognise that.

USEFUL ORGANISATIONS

Age Concern
Bernard Sunley House, Pitcairn Road, Mitcham, Surrey
CR4 3LL.
Tel: 01–640 5431

Alzheimer's Disease Society
158–160 Balham High Street, London SW12 9BN.
Tel: 01–675 6557/8/9

The Association of Continence Advisors
c/o The Disabled Living Foundation, 380–384 Harrow
Road, London W9 2HU.
Tel: 01–289 6111

The Association of Crossroads Care Schemes
10 Regent Place, Rugby, Warwickshire, CV21 2PN.
Tel: (0788) 73653

CancerLink
46 Pentonville Road, London N1 9HF.
Tel: 01–833 2451

Carers National Association
29 Chilworth Mews, London W2 3RG.
Tel: 01–724 7776

The Chest, Heart and Stroke Association
Tavistock House North, Tavistock Square, London WC1H
9JE.
Tel: 01–387 3012

Contact-a-Family
16 Strutton Ground, London SW1P 2HP
Tel: 01–222 2695

Counsel and Care for the Elderly
Twyman House, Lower Ground Floor, 16 Bonny Street, London NW1 9BG.
Tel: 01–485 1550

Holiday Care Service
2 Old Bank Chambers, Station Road, Horley, Surrey RH6 9HW.
Tel: (0293) 774535

Mencap (The Royal Society for Mentally Handicapped Children and Adults)
123 Golden Lane, London EC1Y 0RT.
Tel: 01–253 9433

MIND
22 Harley Street, London W1N 2EN.
Tel: 01–637 0741

The Multiple Sclerosis Society of Great Britain and Northern Ireland
25 Effie Road, Fulham, London SW6 1EE.
Tel: 01–736 6267/8

Parkinson's Disease Society
36 Portland Place, London W1
Tel: 01–323 1174

RADAR (Royal Association for Disability and Rehabilitation)
25 Mortimer Street, London W1N 8AB.
Tel: 01–637 5400

Relate (formerly Marriage Guidance Council)
Herbert Gray College, Little Church Street, Rugby, Warwickshire CV21 3HP.
Tel: (0788) 73241

REFERENCES AND FURTHER READING

AUDIT COMMISSION (1986). *Making a Reality of Community Care*, HMSO.

GARTLEY, C. B. (1988). *Managing Incontinence*, Souvenir Press.

GREEN, H. (1988). *Informal Carers*, HMSO.

GRIFFITHS, Sir R. (1988). *Community Care — An Agenda for Action*, HMSO.

HICKS, C. (1988). *Who Cares: Looking After People at Home*, Virago Press.

KOHNER, N. *Caring at Home*, King's Fund/Informal Caring Programme.

LEWIS, J., and MEREDITH, B. *Daughters Who Care*, Routledge & Kegan Paul.

MACE, N., et al. *The 36 Hour Day*, Age Concern.

PULLING, J. *The Caring Trap*, Fontana Books.

RICHARDSON, A. *A New Deal for Carers*, King's Fund/Informal Caring Programme.

UNGERSON, C. (1987). *Policy is Personal*, Tavistock Publications.

WAGNER, G. (1988). *A Positive Choice*, HMSO.

WILLMOTT, P. (1986). *Social Networks, Informal Care and Public Policy*, Policy Studies Institute.

WILSON, J. *Caring Together*, King's Fund/Informal Caring Programme.

WOODS, R. T. (1989). *Alzheimer's Disease: Coping with a Living Death*, Souvenir Press.

WRIGHT, F. (1986). *Left to Care Alone*, Gower Press.

Index